PREACHING THE SOCIAL DOCTRINE
OF THE CHURCH IN THE MASS

_____

YEAR A

Preaching the Social Doctrine of the Church in the Mass

Year A

James M. Reinert

Libreria Editrice Vaticana

United States Conference of Catholic Bishops
Washington, DC

First printing, November 2013

Cover image copyright © Shutterstock.

ISBN 978-1-60137-277-2

Contents

Introduction

In his Encyclical Letter *Centesimus Annus*, Pope John Paul II referred to the social doctrine of the Church as a "valid instrument of evangelization" (no. 54). In another part of the Encyclical, he also wrote that: "In effect, to teach and to spread her social doctrine pertains to the Church's evangelizing mission and is an essential part of the Christian message, since this doctrine points out the direct consequences of that message in the life of society and situates daily work and struggles for justice in the context of bearing witness to Christ the Savior" (no. 5).

With this in mind and in the hope of furthering an understanding of the social doctrine of the Church, the Pontifical Council for Justice and Peace has prepared "homily helps" for the Sundays of the liturgical year as well as for the major Solemnities of the Church calendar.

These texts, based upon Scriptural readings and infused with the social teaching of the Church will help guide the homilist in making the connection between the Sacred Scriptures and the world of today. Although some of these texts are lengthy, they are not intended to be "stand-alone homilies" but as a guide for developing homilies throughout the three-year cycle of liturgical years.

These English language "homily helps" have been prepared by Rev. Msgr. James Reinert, PhD, a priest of the Diocese of Lincoln, Nebraska, USA, and an official of the Pontifical Council for Justice and Peace since 2003.

Renato Raffaele Cardinal Martino, President,
The Pontifical Council for Justice and Peace

Vatican City
September 1, 2009

First Sunday of Advent

YEAR "A"

Isaiah 2:1-5 • Romans 13:11-14 • Matthew 24:37-44

Today, we begin the Season of Advent, the time of joyful preparation for the celebration of the revelation of God's love through the Birth of his Son. Advent is a time of reflection on the past and a view toward a new beginning. It is also a time when we contemplate our current situation; the world in which each of us finds ourselves. The message of this First Sunday of Advent offers us a reminder of who we are as members of God's family and how we should respond to the Father's offer of salvation.

The three readings for this First Sunday of Advent provide us with a message of God's providence, mercy, and love. From Isaiah we hear of a promise of God's salvation. In his Letter to the Romans, St. Paul takes up where Jesus left off in the Gospel passage, telling us what we must do in order to be prepared for judgment. In the Gospel of St. Matthew, Jesus foretells what will happen at the end of the world.

Jesus is preparing his disciples for the time when he will be taken from them. Today's reading comes just two chapters before the story of the Last Supper and Passion. Jesus knows that "the day is at hand" and shares a warning with his listeners: "At an hour you do not expect, the Son of Man will come." In telling us this, Jesus cautions us to be watching and ready; to always be prepared to meet the Lord in judgment.

The Prophet Isaiah opened his book with a long explanation of why the people of Israel have found themselves in their current state. They have "forsaken the Lord, / spurned the Holy One of Israel, / apostatized" (1:4).

At the same time, Isaiah shares the message of God's promise, "Wash yourselves clean! / Put away your misdeeds from before my eyes; / cease doing evil / learn to do good. / Make justice your aim: redress the wronged, / hear the orphan's plea, defend the widow" (1:16-17). The Prophet then gives us one of those passages that is so familiar and so closely associated, not only with Isaiah but also with the coming of the Messiah, who, according to the Prophet Micah, "shall be peace" (Mi 5:4): "They shall beat their swords into plowshares / and their spears into pruning hooks; / one nation shall not raise the sword against another, / nor shall they train for war again" (Is 2:4).

The coming of the Messiah will bring a new peace to the world. This should be seen not only as an absence of war but as the "fullness of life." This peace is "one of the greatest gifts that God offers to all men and women, and it involves obedience to the divine plan. Peace is the effect of the blessing that God bestows upon his people" (no. 489).* It is a gift that produces fruitfulness, well-being, prosperity, absence of fear, and profound joy. This peace is a gift that each of us should seek in our lives and in the life of the world.

St. Paul wrote to the community of believers in Rome and reminded them of those words of Jesus, outlining how they are to put the words of the Gospel into practice... to throw off those things that would separate us from the love of God and keep us from the place in the Kingdom that Jesus has prepared for all of us.

Of course, this sums up the message of the Gospel. The Word has become flesh, he has shared his life with us, teaching us of the love of God the Father, offering himself in the Eucharist, suffering, dying, and being raised up for our salvation, preparing the disciples to continue to share the message of his Word and love, and waiting to welcome those who keep his Commandments into his Heavenly Kingdom.

The social doctrine of the Church is based upon that same evangelization. It has developed over time, in response to the world and society. Pope John Paul II called social doctrine "the accurate formulation of the results of a careful reflection on the complex realities of human existence in society

---

* [All in-text citations, unless noted otherwise, refer to the corresponding paragraph in the *Compendium of the Social Doctrine of the Church*.]

and in the international order, in the light of faith and the Church's tradition" (*Sollicitudo Rei Socialis*, no. 41).

Put simply, in a certain sense, the social teaching of the Church is the intersection of Christian life coming into contact with the real world. By uniting faith and reason, there is a universality in social doctrine. It is applicable to all people in all situations. The Church bases its social doctrine on philosophy by which mankind comes to a fuller and deeper understanding of truth. It also uses social and human sciences in order for the teaching of the Church to be "reliable, concrete and relevant." By using the human sciences, the Church is better equipped to "speak the language of mankind" and to help society react to the situations that arise in the world.

Through the social teaching of the Church, the situation in which humanity finds itself is brought to light. We see that the Church actively responds to that situation so that we might continue on this journey.

Just as Isaiah and the other prophets were called to proclaim God's message to the Israelite people, we have been entrusted by Jesus to the care and responsibility of the Church (cf. *Centesimus Annus*, no. 53). Proclaiming the Gospel message of love and preparing each person to share in everlasting life are the ways in which the Church fulfills that ongoing responsibility.

The Immaculate Conception of the Blessed Virgin Mary

Genesis 3:9-15, 20 • *Ephesians 1:3-6, 11-12* • *Luke 1:26-38*

"Lord…you preserved the most Blessed Virgin Mary from all stain of Original Sin." In reality, nothing more needs to be said. This phrase, taken from the Preface of today's Mass, in just a few words, sums up everything that we celebrate today.

In the Book of Genesis, a few verses earlier than today's reading, we find: "God blessed them, saying: / 'Be fertile and multiply; / fill the earth and subdue it. / Have dominion over the fish of the sea, the birds of the air, / and all the living things that move on the earth.'… / And so it happened. / God looked at everything he had made, and he found it very good" (Gn 1:28-31).

There are two very important points here. In the first, God the Father gave our first parents dominion over all of creation. It is important to remember that with the "fall of Adam," "the Creator's plan, the meaning of his creatures—and among these, man, who is called to cultivate and care for creation—remains unaltered" (no. 256).

In the second point the author of the Book of Genesis tells that, now that human beings have been added to creation, it was not simply good…as light and darkness, seas and dry land, fish, birds, and animals have been described…but now, creation is very good.

Adam and Eve have sinned. They have broken the relationship of trust and harmony with God, and their selfishness has caused them to forget that they have "received everything as a free gift and that [they] continue to be a creature and not the Creator. It was precisely this temptation that prompted the sin of Adam and Eve: 'You will be like God' (Gn 3:5). They wanted absolute dominion over all things, without having to submit to the will of the Creator" (no. 256).

All is not lost. God makes the promise, "He will strike at your head, / while you strike at his heel." This is our hope for salvation. However, the relationship of trust and harmony must be established once again. Down through the ages the promise is repeated. Now, the time has come for God's plan for our salvation to be revealed.

In his Letter to the Ephesians, St. Paul rejoices that God "chose us in him . . . In love he destined us for adoption to himself through Jesus Christ . . . for the praise of the glory of his grace / that he granted us in the beloved."

It is clear to see that St. Paul understands the relationship between God and mankind has been healed. In the life, the teaching, the sacrifice, the Passion and Resurrection of Jesus we realize that we have been renewed as the beloved of God because he has adopted us to be his children through Christ.

In St. Luke, we hear the most important words that have ever been spoken. More important than the words of Jesus in the Gospel: "Your sins are forgiven . . . Your faith has saved you / go in peace" (Lk 7:48-50); or, "Take it; this is my body" (Mk 14:22); or, "My Father, if it is possible, / let this cup pass from me; / yet, not as I will, but as you will" (Mt 26:39); or even, "Father, into your hands I commend my spirit" (Lk 23:46).

Yes, the response that Mary makes to the announcement of the angel are the most important words that have ever been spoken. At that moment, as Mary says, "Behold, I am the handmaid of the Lord. / May it be done to me according to your word" (Lk 1:38), the "Word became flesh / and made his dwelling among us" (Jn 1:14). This was the Father's plan. However, none of the words and actions of Jesus could have been heard or seen without that response of faith and trust made in "a town of Galilee named Nazareth, / to a Virgin betrothed to a man named Joseph" (Lk 1:26).

Suddenly we are no longer lost. The promise of God the Father has been fulfilled. The story of salvation takes a dramatic turn as the relationship that mankind once had with God, lost by the sin of Adam and Eve, has been renewed, and we will be saved.

"By her 'fiat' to the plan of God's love (cf. Lk 1:38), in the name of all humanity, Mary accepts in history the One sent by the Father, the Savior of mankind. In her Magnificat she proclaims the advent of the Mystery of Salvation, the coming of the 'Messiah of the poor' (cf. Is 11:4; 61:1). The God of the Covenant, whom the Virgin of Nazareth praises in song as her spirit rejoices, is the One who casts down the mighty from their thrones and raises up the lowly, fills the hungry with good things and sends the rich away empty, scatters the proud and shows mercy to those who fear him (cf. Lk 1:50-53).

"Looking to the heart of Mary, to the depth of her faith expressed in the words of the Magnificat, Christ's disciples are called to renew ever more fully in themselves 'the awareness that the truth about God who saves, the truth about God who is the source of every gift, cannot be separated from the manifestation of his love of preference for the poor and humble; that love which, celebrated in the Magnificat, is later expressed in the words and works of Jesus.'[1] Mary is totally dependent upon God and completely directed toward him by the impetus of her faith. She is 'the most perfect image of freedom and of the liberation of humanity and of the universe'"[2] (no. 59).

Let us pray that we might follow her example every day of our lives.

---

1   John Paul II, Encyclical Letter *Redemptoris Mater*, no. 37: *AAS* 79 (1987), 410.
2   Congregation for the Doctrine of the Faith, Instruction *Libertatis Conscientia*, no. 97: *AAS* 79 (1987), 597.

Second Sunday of Advent

YEAR "A"

Isaiah 11:1-10 • *Romans 15:4-9* • *Matthew 3:1-12*

Today, in a passage from the section of the Book of the Prophet Isaiah known as the *Book of Emanuel*, we are introduced to the promise of the Messiah by God the Father. Through that promise we are called to be people of hope, and we see some of the symbols by which the Kingdom of God will be recognized; signs and symbols that are closely connected to the Advent Season.

In this Second Sunday of Advent, we are also introduced to John the Baptist and his ministry. Just as the images of the coming of the Kingdom of God are so familiar, the image and message of the Baptist are also closely associated with this time of preparation.

In many ways, the Book of the Prophet Isaiah is a book of celebration, promise, and hope. "A shoot shall sprout from the stump of Jesse"—from the family of King David—and "a bud shall blossom." "The Spirit of the LORD shall rest upon him...then the wolf shall be a guest of the lamb."

The people of Israel are in exile, but the Word of God continues to be proclaimed. They are separated from their homes and homeland, from their temple and the land given to their fathers, and yet, the promise remains, and all things will be made new. As dark as the situation might seem, there is still hope.

St. Paul, in his Letter to the Romans, reminds the community that through their faith they are called to live in harmony with one another. He tells them that everything written before their time, everything in the Old Testament, is aimed at giving us hope because of the promise that they contain—a promise that they now see fulfilled in Jesus. He makes this plea to a community made up of different backgrounds and belief traditions. Some are converts from Judaism, and some were Gentiles. Now, they are all Christians and are called to glorify God through the Spirit of Jesus Christ.

If we include the passage from Paul's Letter to the Galatians, "Through faith you are all children of God in Christ Jesus. / For all of you who were baptized into Christ / have clothed yourselves with Christ. / There is neither Jew nor Greek, / there is neither slave nor free person, / there is not male and female; / for you are all one in Christ Jesus" (Gal 3:26-28), we recognize the importance of understanding the conversion that we have been called to undergo.

St. Matthew's description of John the Baptist echoes the description of the Prophet Elijah (2 Kgs 1:8). Elijah was the first of the great prophets called by God to deliver his Word, renew his covenant, and teach the people "to look forward to salvation" (Eucharistic Prayer IV). It was Elijah who proved to the Israelite people that there was only one true God. He was sent to turn the people from their worship of false gods and reconcile them to presence of God in their lives.

Now, the time has come for the new message of God's love as John the Baptist begins his ministry in the desert. All four of the Gospels tell the story of the Baptist and his ministry. He called the people of Judea and Jerusalem and the region around the Jordan to repentance in preparation for the coming of the Messiah.

According to St. Matthew, John's message is the same as that which Jesus preaches during his public ministry: "Repent, for the kingdom of heaven is at hand." The Baptist calls the people to conversion and warns that the time for change is short. That message reminds us of the Gospel from last Sunday where Jesus told his listeners: "Stay awake! / For you do not know on which day your Lord will come" (Mt 24:42).

He also points an accusing finger at the Pharisees and Sadducees for relying upon their tradition and ancestry as "children of Abraham" rather than relying upon true faith. In doing so, the Baptist makes it clear that the message is not his own and that "one mightier than I is coming after me."

According to John the Baptist, his baptism with water is only a symbol. The one to come will provide a Baptism of fire and the spirit. Once again, we are presented with the image of the Last Judgment and the coming of the Kingdom.

As people of hope, we recognize our place in the world with regard to our faith. We have been called to conversion, and the Church provides us with the opportunity to renew ourselves in preparation for that moment when we are called to judgment. Our faith helps us to see "the abysses of sin, but in the light of the hope, greater than any evil, given by Jesus Christ's act of redemption, in which sin and death are destroyed (cf. Rom 5:18-21; 1 Cor 15:56-57): 'In him God reconciled man to himself.'[3] It is Christ, the image of God (cf. 2 Cor 4:4; Col 1:15), who enlightens fully and brings to completion the image and likeness of God in man. The Word that became man in Jesus Christ has always been mankind's life and light, the light that enlightens every person (cf. Jn 1:4, 9). God desires in the one mediator Jesus Christ, his Son, the salvation of all men and women (cf. 1 Tm 2:4-5)" (no. 121).

---

3   John Paul II, Apostolic Exhortation *Reconciliatio et Paenitentia*, no. 10: *AAS* 77 (1965), 205.

Third Sunday of Advent

YEAR "A"

Isaiah 35:1-6, 10 • James 5:7-10 • Matthew 11:2-11

"Who are you?" and "Who do people say that the Son of Man is?" St. Matthew draws us into the two questions here in this passage from Chapter 11, and again in Chapter 16. In the Gospel passage today, however, it is John the Baptist who asked the question, "Are you the one who is to come?"

Jesus answers the Baptist's question in a way that could be seen as more direct and clear. He responds to the question by calling to mind the passage of the promise from the Prophet Isaiah: "Then will the eyes of the blind be opened, / the ears of the deaf be cleared; / then will the lame leap like a stag, / then the tongue of the mute will sing." Here, Jesus includes the promise, "And the poor have the good news proclaimed to them. / And blessed is the one who takes no offense at me." These are the proof that what God the Father has promised has been made real.

Here we see an important revelation. The Kingdom of God will be a time and place when the cares and concerns of those in need will be addressed. Isaiah preaches words of comfort. The promise of God is to relieve the suffering and want of those who are downcast, oppressed, poor, disadvantaged, abandoned, or lost. Jesus speaks the same message. He has come to heal, to forgive, to make strong, and to share the Good News of God's love. Along with that, Jesus calls us to realize that each and every person is our neighbor, and we are called not only to be concerned for our neighbors but also to love them if we are to share in the Kingdom of God.

"In [Jesus] it is always possible to recognize the living sign of that measureless and transcendent love of God-with-us, [Emmanuel] who takes on the infirmities of his people, walks with them, saves them and makes them one.[4] In him and thanks to him, life in society too, despite all its contradictions and ambiguities, can be rediscovered as a place of life and hope, in that it is a sign of grace that is continuously offered to all, and because it is an invitation to ever higher and more involved forms of sharing.

"Jesus of Nazareth makes the connection between solidarity and charity shine brightly before all, illuminating the entire meaning of this connection:[5] 'In the light of faith, solidarity seeks to go beyond itself, to take on the specifically Christian dimensions of total gratuity, forgiveness and reconciliation. One's neighbor is then not only a human being with his or her own rights and a fundamental equality with everyone else, but becomes the living image of God the Father, redeemed by the blood of Jesus Christ and placed under the permanent action of the Holy Spirit. One's neighbor must therefore be loved, even if an enemy, with the same love with which the Lord loves him or her; and for that person's sake one must be ready for sacrifice, even the ultimate one: to lay down one's life for the brethren (cf. 1 Jn 3:16)'"[6] (no. 196).

In Chapter 16 of the Gospel, when Jesus asks a similar question and hears the responses of the disciples, Jesus gives no direct answer. At the same time, however he does let Simon Peter know that he has answered correctly, and that it is God the Father who reveals these things to those with the faith to believe.

The preaching of God's Word is meant to bring about a change in the lives of those who hear it. During this Advent season we hear the Word as a message of comfort and compassion. Everything will be made new as the Kingdom of God is revealed to us. The Kingdom will be revealed by the Messiah, and we are invited to participate in it by the good that we do in our lives.

---

4   Cf. Second Vatican Ecumenical Council, Pastoral Constitution *Gaudium et Spes*, no. 32: *AAS* 58 (1966), 1051.

5   Cf. John Paul II, Encyclical Letter *Sollicitudo Rei Socialis*, no. 40: *AAS* 80 (1988), 568: "*Solidarity* is undoubtedly a *Christian virtue*. In what has been said so far it has been possible to identify many points of contact between solidarity and *charity*, which is the distinguishing mark of Christ's disciples (cf. Jn 13:35)."

6   John Paul II, Encyclical Letter *Sollicitudo Rei Socialis*, no. 40: *AAS* 80 (1988), 569.

"Christ the Savior showed compassion in this regard, identifying himself with the 'least' among men (cf. Mt 25:40, 45). 'It is by what they have done for the poor that Jesus Christ will recognize his chosen ones. When "the poor have the good news preached to them" (Mt 11:5), it is a sign of Christ's presence'"[7] (no. 183).

The Prophet Isaiah continues to preach words of comfort and patience to the people of Israel. He tells them of the wonders of the Father's love and the glories that they will see when his promise is fulfilled. Isaiah also lets them know that fulfillment is not something "far off." Rather, he proclaims, "Here is your God, / he comes with vindication."

In his Letter, St. James shares the same message of encouragement, "Be patient, brothers and sisters...Make your hearts firm, / because the coming of the Lord is at hand."

Today's readings help us to understand why we should keep patient watch. They enable us to realize who this promised Messiah is and what his coming will mean in our lives as he renews himself in our hearts.

Jesus is the Messiah, the fulfillment of the promise of salvation that God the Father has made down through the ages. In this Third Sunday of Advent the preparations for greeting the Birth of Christ should be well under-way. Soon, the Church will add the "O Antiphons" to her prayers. In a way, these help us to deepen our understanding and give clarity to our response in answering the question, "Are you the one?": O Wisdom of God; O Ruler of Israel; O Root of Jesse; O Key of David; O Dawn of light; O King of the Nations; O Emmanuel!

---

7   *Catechism of the Catholic Church*, no. 2443.

Jesus' Paschal Mystery, so that his old self, with its evil inclinations, is cruci-fied with Christ. As a new creation he is then enabled by grace to 'walk in newness of life' (Rom 6:4). This 'holds true not for Christians alone but also for all people of good will in whose hearts grace is active invisibly. For since Christ died for all, and since all men are in fact called to one and the same destiny, which is divine, we must hold that the Holy Spirit offers to all the possibility of being made partners, in a way known to God, in the Paschal Mystery'"[34] (no. 41).

---

[34]   Second Vatican Ecumenical Council, Pastoral Constitution *Gaudium et Spes*, no. 22: *AAS* 58 (1966), 1043.

The Third Sunday of Lent

YEAR "A"

Exodus 17:3-7 • *Romans 5:1-2, 5-8* • *John 4:5-42*

God provides the Israelite people with water from a rock. This is only one incident in which the people doubt the presence of God and grumble against him and Moses. It is also an occasion when God shows his presence and power.

The people are reminded that it was God who freed them from their slavery. It was God who led them through the Red Sea and guided them through the desert. It was God who feeds them when they are hungry and gives them water when they thirst. One might think that the only explanation for the reaction of the Israelites is that they do not know for what or to whom to look as they search for God's presence.

They saw the pillar of cloud and the fire that led them day and night on their journey. They heard his thunder on the mountain when they were given the Ten Commandments. They saw how Moses, at God's instruction, held out his staff and the Red Sea was split so that they could walk on dry land through the midst of the sea. Now they have seen how, once again at God's instruction, Moses strikes the stone from which water began to flow.

Still, they have not actually seen God. They may have heard his thunder but they have not heard his voice.

"Is the LORD in our midst or not?" The question is asked at the end of the First Reading and appears to have been on the lips of the people throughout their forty years of wandering in the desert.

The answer came in St. Paul's Letter to the Romans, where he wrote: "Therefore, since we have been justified by faith, / we have peace with God through our Lord Jesus Christ." He has found great success in his preaching. His months in the city of Corinth were fruitful in establishing a strong Christian community. Now he writes to encourage the Church in Rome, telling them of the great gifts that have been given to them through the Spirit. These gifts transcend anything that the world might give.

St. Paul heard the voice of the Lord while on the road to Damascus. Later, he learned of the gospel message that Jesus preached. He put his faith in Jesus and the salvation that he won for us through his suffering, Death, and Resurrection. After that, he set himself to preaching and teaching that message of redemption, justification, and salvation. There is a confidence and a sense of comfort and possibly relief in St. Paul's words today. "But God proves his love for us / in that while we were still sinners Christ died for us." He goes on to state: "How much more then, since we are now justified by his blood, / will we be saved through him from the wrath."

Lent is a time for us to be reminded of those very facts: that while we were still sinners, while we were still asking, "Is God present in our life?" the Father sent his Son to live among us, to teach us of his love and who suffered and died for us to prove that love.

In the Gospel, we have the wonderful story of the "woman at the well." There are a few similarities with the story involving Elijah in 1 Kings 17:8-24 that are worth noting.

Elijah, the first great prophet of Israel, called out to the widow of Zarephath and said, "Bring me a little water in a vessel, that I may drink," and at the end of the story, after Elijah has performed miracles for her and her son, the widow proclaims: "Now indeed I know that you are a man of God. / The word of the LORD comes truly from your mouth."

Jesus asked the Samaritan woman for a drink, spoke to her about her life, and invited her to share in the water that he will give…which will become in her a spring welling up to eternal life. After all of this, she professes her faith: "I know that the Christ is coming…when he comes, he will tell us everything."

Not only do we hear her profession of faith but we also see that she has become a disciple of the Word. She told the people of her village, and St. John tells us that because of her word, her testimony, many came to believe in Jesus, and many more came to believe through the words that Jesus spoke to them.

As Pope John Paul II said to a group of bishops from the United States: "Pastors must honestly ask whether they have paid sufficient attention to the thirst of the human heart for the true 'living water' which only Christ our Redeemer can give (cf. Jn 4:7-13)." Like him, we want to rely "on the perennial freshness of the Gospel message and its capacity to transform and renew those who accept it" (cf. no. 463).

Just as in the words of St. Paul in his Letter to the Romans, we should have the same sense of confidence, comfort, and relief. We have the Gospel message through which we share in the living waters that become for us a spring of salvation. In a few weeks, on Holy Saturday and the Vigil Mass, we will celebrate the blessing of the font and the renewal of our Baptismal promises. Let us pray that the life-giving waters will truly be a sign of the redemption that has come to us through our faith in Jesus, our life.

The Fourth Sunday of Lent
YEAR "A"

1 Samuel 16:1b, 4a, 6-7, 10-13a • *Ephesians 5:8-14* • *John 9:1-41*

The Son of God is the Messiah, the Anointed One; he came into the world to be our light! Today's readings could be summarized in that phrase. The readings are filled with images that focus upon the one who has been chosen and the light that dispels darkness.

The reading from the Book of Samuel is straightforward. Samuel is sent by God to anoint David as the new king of Israel. At first, Samuel is reluctant, fearing that King Saul will hear the news. This anointing is significant, because it symbolized being chosen by God. God's favor has now fallen upon David, his anointed one. The words "Messiah" and "Christ" mean "the anointed one"—"the one chosen by God."

David was the chosen one of God, "and from that day on, the spirit of the LORD rushed upon David." He was chosen as king over the Israelite people. It would be David who would make Jerusalem the capital of Israel after he brought peace to the land; from his lineage the Messiah would come.

Here it is important to point out an interesting fact: David had no choice in the matter. He was chosen by God…he was anointed. However, once he was chosen, he responded to God's call.

"David is the recipient of the promise (cf. 2 Sm 7:13-16; Ps 89:2-38; 132:11-18), which places him at the beginning of a special kingly tradition, the 'messianic' tradition. Notwithstanding all the sins and infidelities of David and his successors, this tradition culminates in Jesus Christ, who is *par excellence* 'Yahweh's anointed' (that is, 'the Lord's consecrated one,' cf. 1 Sm 2:35; 24:7, 11; 26:9, 16; Ex 30:22-32), the son of David (cf. Mt 1:1-17; Lk 3:23-38; Rom 1:3)" (no. 378).

The last line in today's Gospel passage provides us with an interesting contrast to being chosen. We have this long story of the reaction to the miracle that Jesus performed for the man who had been born blind. At the end of the story, we hear Jesus say to the Pharisees, "If you were blind, you would have no sin; / but now you are saying, 'We see,' so your sin remains."

In the *Prologue* to his Gospel, St. John has already told us that the Word of God, who was with God in the beginning, is "the light [that] shines in the darkness, / and the darkness has not overcome it." St. John went on to write: "But to those who did accept him / he gave power to become children of God, / to those who believe in his name, / who were born not by natural generation / nor by human choice nor by a man's decision / but of God." "Not by natural generation / nor by human choice." Does that not sound familiar? Chosen by God—now, how will he respond?

Jesus has come as the "light of the world" and invites us to share in that light. For those who accept, for those who follow, the light dispels the darkness of ignorance and sin. For those who refuse to accept the light, they are condemned to darkness and place themselves outside the Kingdom of Heaven.

Jesus assured his disciples that the man "blind from birth" was not blind because of sin but rather, so that "the works of God might be made visible through him." This will be not just a miracle of healing, but it will also be a teaching moment. Just as in last week's story of the "woman at the well," when the man who was blind experienced the love of Jesus and the presence of the Spirit of God in him, he made a profession of faith. Jesus asks: "'Do you believe in the Son of Man?' / He answered and said, / 'Who is he, sir, that I may believe in him?' / Jesus said to him, 'You have seen him, and / the one speaking with you is he.' / He said, / 'I do believe, Lord,' and he worshiped him."

We know that we have been chosen. We are invited to walk in the light of faith. We have been given a share in the Kingdom. Now, it is our turn to respond to all of this. During this Season of Lent we are reminded how important that response is in this life and the life to come.

St. Paul addressed that response in his Letter to the Ephesians. He encouraged the community to "live as children of light" and to "try to learn what is pleasing to the Lord." At the same time, St. Paul warned against the dangers of falling into darkness.

"Christians, particularly the laity, are urged to act in such a way that 'the power of the Gospel might shine forth in their daily social and family life. They conduct themselves as children of the promise and thus strong in faith and hope they make the most of the present (cf. Eph 5:16; Col 4:5), and with patience await the glory that is to come (cf. Rom 8:25). Let them not, then, hide this hope in the depths of their hearts, but let them express it by a continual conversion and by wrestling "against the world-rulers of this darkness, against the spiritual forces of wickedness" (Eph 6:12).'[35] The religious motivation behind such a commitment may not be shared by all, but the moral convictions that arise from it represent a point of encounter between Christians and all people of good will" (no. 579).

---

35   Second Vatican Ecumenical Council, Dogmatic Constitution *Lumen Gentium*, no. 35: *AAS* 57 (1965), 40.

The Fifth Sunday of Lent

YEAR "A"

Ezekiel 37:12-14 • Romans 8:8-11 • John 11:1-45

Today it is important to be again reminded of the passage from St. Matthew, when the disciples of John the Baptist are sent to Jesus and asked, "Are you he who is to come, / or should we look for another?" In reply Jesus answered, "Go and tell John what you hear and see: / the blind regain their sight, / the lame walk" (Mt 11:2-6). Of course, this is part of the prophecy of the coming of the Messiah from the Prophet Isaiah (35:5-6). Now, the Prophet Ezekiel adds to those signs, "Then you shall know that I am the LORD, / when I open your graves and have you rise from them, / O my people!"

One must wonder why more people in Jesus' time did not realize the events that they were witnessing were the fulfillment of the promises that God had made. The whole history of salvation up to that point was based upon those promises. The stories surrounding the promises should have been very familiar, especially to the religious authorities of the day. Yet, when they witness them as a reality (the blind see, the lame walk, the dead raised) the majority turned their backs on Jesus rather than place their faith in him.

At the same time, while we discuss new life and being raised from the grave, St. Paul, in his Letter to the Romans, tells us that as long as we have the Spirit of God within us, the body is not important, "But if Christ is in you, / although the body is dead because of sin, / the spirit is alive because of righteousness."

Just as three weeks ago, with the account of the Transfiguration, the story of the raising of Lazarus helps us to prepare for the celebration of the Passion and Death of Jesus. Not only that, but in this passage from St. John we see another profession of faith, "Yes, Lord. / I have come to believe that you are the Christ, the Son of God, / the one who is coming into the world" (11:27), just as we heard from the man who was blind from birth and the woman at the well. What we also see today, as in the story of the woman at the well, is that others become believers after encountering Jesus or learning about his words and work.

Again, the encounter with Jesus calls for a response, and once again we must look within ourselves, as we have been doing in a special way during the Lenten season, in order to find how well we are prepared to respond to meeting Christ each moment of every day.

It is interesting to note the words of Jesus—first to his disciples as he prepares to travel to Bethany, "Lazarus has died. / And I am glad for you that I was not there, / that you may believe." Later, after he arrived, Jesus tells Martha, "I am the resurrection and the life; / whoever believes in me, even if he dies, will live, / and everyone who lives and believes in me will never die." Finally, at the tomb, Jesus prayed, "Father; I thank you for hearing me. / I know that you always hear me; / but because of the crowd here I have said this, / that they may believe that you sent me."

From the beginning, we see that Jesus knew what he was going to do and why he was going to do it. What we do not see is any hesitation or doubt. Jesus knew that he would and that he could raise Lazarus.

"Jesus Christ, however, 'by suffering for us...not only gave us an example so that we might follow in his footsteps, but he also opened up a way. If we follow this path, life and death are made holy and acquire a new meaning.'[36] Christ's disciple adheres, in faith and through the sacraments, to Jesus' Paschal Mystery, so that his *old self*, with its evil inclinations, is crucified with Christ. As a new creation he is then enabled by grace to 'walk in newness of life' (Rom 6:4). This 'holds true not for Christians alone but also for all people of good will in whose hearts grace is active invisibly. For since Christ died for all, and since all men are in fact called to one and the same destiny, which is

---

36   Second Vatican Ecumenical Council, Pastoral Constitution *Gaudium et Spes*, no. 22: *AAS* 58 (1966), 1043.

divine, we must hold that the Holy Spirit offers to all the possibility of being made partners, in a way known to God, in the Paschal Mystery'"[37] (no. 41).

Jesus is the way, the truth, and the life. Through his suffering and Death, he opened the way for us to share in everlasting life. Through his Passion and Resurrection, we are made new, we are changed. Jesus has been preparing his disciples not only for this moment but for the events to come. In raising Lazarus, he shows that he too will rise and that we can join him.

---

37   Second Vatican Ecumenical Council, Pastoral Constitution *Gaudium et Spes*, no. 22: *AAS* 58 (1966), 1043.

Palm Sunday of the Passion of the Lord

YEAR "A"

Matthew 21:1-11 • Isaiah 50:4-7 • Philippians 2:6-11
Matthew 26:14–27:66

"This is Jesus the prophet, from Nazareth in Galilee." "Blessed is he who comes in the name of the Lord!"

St. Matthew uses the prophecy of Zechariah in his description of Jesus' entrance into Jerusalem. What is interesting about that prophecy is the contrast: "Rejoice heartily, O daughter Zion, / shout for joy, O daughter Jerusalem! / See, your king shall come to you; / a just savior is he, / meek, and riding on an ass, / on a colt, the foal of an ass" (9:9).

One might ask whether it is possible to be triumphant and victorious and at the same time humble. By choosing to enter Jerusalem in the manner in which he did, Jesus showed the people the type of king he truly is. He comes in triumph but not triumphantly. He has taught as a shepherd, not as a general. Those who have heard him speak or witnessed a miracle that he worked have now been called to give witness to their experiences. They do so by proclaiming Jesus the "Son of David," praising God the Father for sending their long-awaited savior.

At the same time, however, the religious as well as the political and military authorities must have taken notice of what was happening. Matthew tells us that "the whole city was shaken." The clamor reached their ears, and they responded. St. Matthew does not tell us here, but one can only imagine that their reaction was negative.

According to St. Matthew, Jesus certainly knew the significance of what he was preparing to do. He sent his disciples to fetch the donkey and her colt, explaining in great detail what will happen. As we journey with Jesus and the Apostles over the next few days, we will see a number of images that will remind us of the fact that Jesus, the Son of David, has come to save us and set us free.

It is interesting to note that, according to the Synoptic Gospels, this entrance into Jerusalem is not immediately followed by the story of the Passion. In St. Matthew there are five chapters separating the entrance from the account of the Last Supper.

The triumphant entrance into Jerusalem is tempered a bit and refocused by the passage from the Book of the Prophet Isaiah. We hear of the "Servant of the Lord"—the second of Isaiah's three prophecies that spoke of the Messiah. In those passages we come to understand the true nature of the Messiah—not appearing as a king in glory but as a humble servant.

St. Paul, in his Letter to the Philippians, reinforces that understanding. In the beautiful "Philippians hymn," he tells us who this Jesus really is and what he has done for us, "he humbled himself, / becoming obedient to the point of death, / even death on a cross." All of this shows us that this is all part of God's plan. The Old Testament promises are fulfilled, and we become witnesses. As witnesses we are also called to respond.

"In him it is always possible to recognize the living sign of that measureless and transcendent love of God-with-us, who takes on the infirmities of his people, walks with them, saves them and makes them one.[38] In him and thanks to him, life in society too, despite all its contradictions and ambiguities, can be rediscovered as a place of life and hope, in that it is a sign of grace that is continuously offered to all and because it is an invitation to ever higher and more involved forms of sharing.

---

38   Cf. Second Vatican Ecumenical Council, Pastoral Constitution *Gaudium et Spes*, no. 32: *AAS* 58 (1966), 1051.

"Jesus of Nazareth makes the connection between solidarity and charity shine brightly before all, illuminating the entire meaning of this connection:[39] 'In the light of faith, solidarity seeks to go beyond itself, to take on the specifically Christian dimensions of total gratuity, forgiveness and reconciliation. One's neighbor is then not only a human being with his or her own rights and a fundamental equality with everyone else, but becomes the living image of God the Father, redeemed by the blood of Jesus Christ and placed under the permanent action of the Holy Spirit. One's neighbor must therefore be loved, even if an enemy, with the same love with which the Lord loves him or her; and for that person's sake one must be ready for sacrifice, even the ultimate one: to lay down one's life for the brethren (cf. 1 Jn 3:16)'"[40] (no. 196).

In hearing the account of the Passion according to St. Matthew, which begins with the agreement for his betrayal and ends with Pilate telling the authorities to guard the tomb, we see the Old Testament prophecies in a new light. We also see the events surrounding the Passion, beginning with the account of the Last Supper and the institution of the Eucharist, conform with the pastoral ministry of Jesus. He has come to us and offered a great gift. If we accept that gift we are called to respond to him in his Passion, Death, and Resurrection.

---

39   Cf. John Paul II, Encyclical Letter *Sollicitudo Rei Socialis*, no. 40: *AAS* 80 (1988), 568: "*Solidarity* is undoubtedly a *Christian virtue*. In what has been said so far it has been possible to identify many points of contact between solidarity and *charity*, which is the distinguishing mark of Christ's disciples (cf. Jn 13:35)."

40   John Paul II, Encyclical Letter *Sollicitudo Rei Socialis*, no. 40: *AAS* 80 (1988), 569.

Holy Thursday

MASS OF THE LORD'S SUPPER

Exodus 12:1-8, 11-14 • 1 Corinthians 11:23-26 • John 13:1-15

As we celebrate the Mass of the Lord's Supper and hear the three readings it is important to be reminded of the message found in the three readings from last Sunday (Mt 21:1-11—the story of Jesus' entrance into Jerusalem, Isaiah 50:4-7—the story of the "Servant of the Lord," and Philippians 2:6-11—the life and gift of Jesus who humbled himself and accepted death on a Cross). The heart of this celebration can be better seen by recalling the readings that surround it; those from Palm Sunday and those that will be used on Friday, Saturday, and Sunday.

We also need to be reminded of the fact that even though we heard from the narrative of the Last Supper from the Gospel of St. John, we heard the story of the Institution of the Eucharist from St. Paul's First Letter to the Corinthians. The key element in St. John's account is Jesus' washing of the feet of the Apostles and saying, "I have given you a model to follow, / so that as I have done, you should also do." The celebrations on Passion Sunday and Holy Thursday remind us of the humility of Jesus who has come to us not as a king but as a servant.

In washing the feet of the Apostles, Jesus also provides a lesson on Baptism…of being cleansed and giving "new birth." Water is introduced as an essential element that we will follow through the next few days, especially in the celebration of the Easter Vigil, the blessing of the font, and the renewal of our Baptismal promises (as well as the Baptisms that may take place as part of the Vigil).

"The principle of the universal destination of goods also applies naturally to water, considered in the Sacred Scriptures as a symbol of purification (cf. Ps 51:4; Jn 13:8) and of life (cf. Jn 3:5; Gal 3:27). 'As a gift from God, water is a vital element essential to survival; thus, everyone has a right to it.'[41] Satisfying the needs of all, especially of those who live in poverty, must guide the use of water and of the services connected with it. Inadequate access to safe drinking water affects the well-being of a huge number of people and is often the cause of disease, suffering, conflicts, poverty and even death. For a suitable solution to this problem, it 'must be set in context in order to establish moral criteria based precisely on the value of life and the respect for the rights and dignity of all human beings'"[42] (no. 484).

Finally, along with all of this, in a certain sense, we should be grateful for the selfishness and possible ignorance of the Christian community in Corinth. They are being scolded by St. Paul, and in doing so, he gives us the earliest written account of Jesus sharing his Body and Blood in the form of bread and wine.

The reading from the Book of Exodus tells the story of the Passover event. We see the images that are so familiar to us: the lamb, the unleavened bread, the walking staff, the blood on the doorposts, and the dark of night. The Israelites who follow the directions given to Moses will be "passed-over" this night, and the story of their being freed from their slavery will take a dramatic turn. We will hear of the next great act that secured their freedom on Saturday during the celebration of the Easter Vigil liturgy—the story of the Israelites passing through the Red Sea.

This evening we have the stories of the Passover and the Eucharist. Tomorrow we will read St. John's account of the Passion of Jesus, and on Saturday and Sunday we will hear the account of the Resurrection. The Passion ties the three stories together. The offering, the sacrifice, and the gift of new life are the guarantees of our salvation.

---

41   John Paul II, Message to Cardinal Geraldo Majella Agnelo on the occasion of the 2004 Brotherhood Campaign of the Brazilian Bishops' Conference (January 19, 2004): L'Osservatore Romano, English edition, March 17, 2004, p. 3.

42   John Paul II, Message to Cardinal Geraldo Majella Agnelo on the occasion of the 2004 Brotherhood Campaign of the Brazilian Bishops' Conference (January 19, 2004): L'Osservatore Romano, English edition, March 17, 2004, p. 3.

Easter Sunday of the Resurrection of the Lord

YEAR "A"

Acts 10:34, 37-43 • *Colossians 3:1-4* • *John 20:1-9*

"He saw and believed." Just as we heard in the Gospel readings leading up to this celebration of the Resurrection of Jesus, we once again hear of the reaction to something Jesus has done. St. John provides us with a detailed account of what took place that first Easter Sunday morning. At the end of the passage, he tells us that the disciple whom Jesus loved believed in what he had seen.

In the First Reading, from the Acts of the Apostles, St. Peter summarizes the Gospel message in a few short verses. It is plain to see that he was speaking to people who already knew the story surrounding Jesus of Nazareth—from the beginning of his public ministry to his Resurrection and Ascension. St. Peter also attempts to establish the fact that Jesus intended his ministry and the spreading of the Gospel message to continue through the Apostles.

The three readings provide us with a link between the Resurrection, the empty tomb, and today's celebration. Through the teachings and traditions of the Church, handed down to us by the Apostles, we not only hear the story of Jesus, but we become sharers in it. St. Paul reminds us of this connection in his Letter to the Colossians. He tells the community to rise above the world, because through the Death and Resurrection of Jesus we have been given "new life."

"At the dawn of this Third Millennium, the Church does not tire of proclaiming the Gospel that brings salvation and genuine freedom also to temporal realities. She is mindful of the solemn exhortation given by St. Paul to his disciple Timothy: 'Preach the word, be urgent in season and out of season, convince, rebuke, and exhort, be unfailing in patience and in teaching' (2 Tm 4:2-5)" (no. 2).

"In fact, when the Church 'fulfills her mission of proclaiming the Gospel, she bears witness to man, in the name of Christ, to his dignity and his vocation to the communion of persons. She teaches him the demands of justice and peace in conformity with divine wisdom.'[43] *This doctrine has its own profound unity, which flows from Faith in a whole and complete salvation, from Hope in a fullness of justice, and from Love which makes all mankind truly brothers and sisters in Christ*: it is the expression of God's love for the world, which he so loved 'that he gave his only Son' (Jn 3:16). The new law of love embraces the entire human family and knows no limits, since the proclamation of the salvation wrought by Christ extends 'to the end of the earth' (Acts 1:8)" (no. 3).

During this celebration of the Resurrection of Jesus, we renew our Baptismal promises. In the Introductory Prayer for the ritual, the Celebrant reminds us that "through the Paschal Mystery we have been buried with Christ in Baptism, so that we may walk with him in newness of life."

We rejoice in the empty tomb. We know, however, that Jesus was not taken from there and that we are not alone. Rather, Jesus was raised to new life. With the promise of eternal life, Jesus is with us and has given us the Church to carry out his ministry.

---

43   *Catechism of the Catholic Church*, no. 2419.

Second Sunday of Easter

YEAR "A"

Acts 2:42-47 • *1 Peter 1:3-9* • *John 20:19-31*

"Although you have not seen him you love him; / even though you do not see him now yet you believe in him" (1 Pt 1:8).

Essentially, the passage from the Acts of the Apostles comes after what one might see as a long introduction to the book. St. Luke tells us the story of the formation of the early Church—the community of believers living in Jerusalem. If we turn back that page, we see the commissioning of the Apostles by Jesus, his Ascension, the replacement of Judas by Matthias, the coming of the Holy Spirit, and Peter's Pentecost discourse. It is as if Luke has already set the stage for us and introduces us to the actors. Now, "as the curtain opens," the drama begins.

St. Luke tells us about "the brethren." He casually reveals their lives as believers—how they lived in their community of belief and purpose. This is the first generation of Jesus' followers. There were those who actually witnessed the work and teaching of Jesus, and there were also those who came to believe as a result of what they heard from the Apostles. At the end of the passage, St. Luke tells us that through the instruction of the Apostles and example of the community, the numbers grew each day. He also helps us to recognize that all of this came as a result of the graces poured out by the Holy Spirit.

In his First Letter, St. Peter spoke of that grace and the "new birth" that the community must continue to experience and share. The tone of the Letter is in many ways similar to that of the reading from Acts. It is almost as if St. Peter is giving the members of the community the reason why they live and act in the ways they do. He speaks of trials, but he also speaks of the glory that is to come, all the while celebrating the gift of faith and encouraging his readers to rejoice with him.

This section of St. Peter's Letter was written to the Christian communities as they continue to increase. As time passes, the eye witnesses of the public ministry of Jesus became fewer and fewer. The vast majority of the members of these communities are those who have heard the Gospel message second and thirdhand. St. Peter congratulates these converts and exhorts them to remain faithful to what they have been taught—to live their faith.

All of us share in that teaching. We are those who are "blessed because we believe without seeing."

On the night before he died, Jesus offered his disciples the gift of peace. When he appeared in the Upper Room, he offered that gift of peace a second and third time. He also gave them the gift of the Holy Spirit so that they could finally understand.

St. John tells us that all of these things have been recorded to help us in our faith and that we might have life—a sharing in Jesus' new life. Through the Gospel of St. John we realize that the Church is a community of love based upon the gift of peace and striving for the good of all. We come to know our own "completeness" as individuals and community through the redeeming love of Jesus Christ. This love makes us whole and calls us to be like the people of the early Church, devoting our lives toward evangelization, harmony, and prayer (cf. nos. 65, 159, 164, 166).

Third Sunday of Easter

YEAR "A"

Acts 2:14, 22-28 • *1 Peter 1:17-21* • *Luke 24:13-35*

Today's passage from the Acts of the Apostles is an account of the first part of St. Peter's Pentecost discourse and actually precedes the reading that we had last week in which St. Luke described the early Church community. In it, St. Luke described how St. Peter told of the Passion and Resurrection of Jesus and shared his understanding of the plan for salvation laid out by God the Father. He draws from the image of King David in the Old Testament, referring to the sixteenth Psalm as a proof of the Resurrection and for our hope of not being abandoned by the Father. (Parts of that Psalm are used for today's Responsorial Psalm.)

In that passage, St. Luke places us in Jerusalem as the crowds gathered in wonder over the sign that was presented to them; each of them hears the preaching of the Apostles in their own native language. Now, empowered by the gifts of the Holy Spirit, Peter steps forward and speaks to the people. He wants them to understand their role in God's plan as well as make a connection between the Israelites coming out of Egypt and receiving the Ten Commandments on Mt. Sinai with the signs and wonders that are taking place now.

St. Peter continues that idea in today's Second Reading from the First Letter of Peter. In it, he drew a parallel with the Israelites wandering in the desert before coming to the Promised Land and life in the present day. The Christian converts, who are the recipients of this Letter, are encouraged to truly separate themselves from their pagan ways of life of their past. They are also reminded that they have been saved at a great cost; and because of that, they believe and are now people of hope.

"The Church teaches men and women that God offers them the real possibility of overcoming evil and of attaining good. The Lord has redeemed mankind 'bought with a price' (1 Cor 6:20). The meaning and basis of the Christian commitment in the world are founded on this certainty, which gives rise to hope despite the sin that deeply marks human history: the divine promise guarantees that the world does not remain closed in upon itself but is open to the Kingdom of God. The Church knows the effects of 'the mystery of lawlessness' (2 Thes 2:7), but she also knows that 'there exist in the human person sufficient qualities and energies, a fundamental "goodness" (cf. Gn 1:31), because he is the image of the Creator, placed under the redemptive influence of Christ, who "united himself in some fashion with every man," and because the efficacious action of the Holy Spirit "fills the earth" (Wis 1:7)'"[44] (no. 578).

St. Luke ties all of those ideas together in the story of the disciples traveling to Emmaus. This stranger whom they encounter but do not recognize as Jesus opens their minds to the Scriptures and explains how all the events of the past three days were part of God's plan. Even then they still did not recognize their companion as Jesus. It was only in the breaking of the bread that "their eyes were opened."

St. Luke is the only Evangelist that tells us this story of "other disciples" encountering Jesus after the Resurrection. It must have been a terribly hectic day with the various reports of Jesus being seen—with the disciples going from one place to another, with the hope that the stories were true and that Jesus might still be present.

It must also have been a very trying day as everyone who heard the reports struggled to make sense of the information that was given to them. These two disciples mulled over those events as they discussed and made their way to Emmaus. However, it was only when Jesus opened their minds that they understood, even as their hearts "burned inside them."

Last Sunday we heard that in the days following the Ascension of Jesus, the Apostles "devoted themselves...to the breaking of bread and to the

---

44   John Paul II, Encyclical Letter *Sollicitudo Rei Socialis*, no. 47: *AAS* 80 (1988), 580.

prayers." They realized that in that celebration of the commemoration of the Lord's Supper and in their communal prayer, Jesus was truly present.

The Church continues to understand his presence in our prayers and celebration of the Sacraments, especially the Eucharist. Jesus has opened our minds to God the Father's plan for our salvation. As our hearts burn within us in our love for Christ, we are called to live as community; to shed the old ways and celebrate the new life that we have been given through his Death and Resurrection.

"Salvation, which the Lord Jesus obtained 'at a price' (1 Cor 6:20; cf. 1 Pt 1:18-19), is achieved in the new life that awaits the righteous after death, but it also permeates this world in the realities of the economy and labor, of technology and communications, of society and politics, of the international community and the relations among cultures and peoples. 'Jesus came to bring integral salvation, one which embraces the whole person and all mankind, and opens up the wondrous prospect of divine filiation'"[45] (no. 1).

In a way, this Easter season is not only the celebration of our salvation through the Death and Resurrection of Jesus, it should also be seen as a time for our preparation for the celebration of Pentecost—when we commemorate the coming of the Holy Spirit and the courage and understanding that his gifts bring to us.

---

45   John Paul II, Encyclical Letter *Redemptoris Missio*, no. 11: *AAS* 83 (1991), 260.

Fourth Sunday of Easter

YEAR "A"

Acts 2:14a, 36-41 • 1 Peter 2:20-25 • John 10:1-10

"The Lord is my shepherd; there is nothing I shall want." The Psalm response for today's Liturgy is rich in its images.

In the reading from the Acts of the Apostles, we hear the second part of St. Peter's Pentecost discourse. In speaking to the crowd gathered outside the house where the disciples had gathered, Peter has already established their understanding of who Jesus was and what happened to him. St. Peter spoke first of the human Jesus. Now, he speaks of Jesus as Messiah, Lord, and Son of God.

Once the attention of the crowd is focused upon this fact, there is a change in their attitude. They no longer question the validity of the argument. Instead, they respond by asking, "What are we to do, my brothers?"

The same question was asked by the crowds that came to the Jordan River to hear the Baptist. At that time he told them, "I am baptizing you with water, / but one mightier than I is coming…He will baptize you with the Holy Spirit and fire" (3:16).

The answer that Peter gives is the same answer that the Church has been giving through the ages to those who wish to follow Jesus: "Repent and be baptized, every one of you, / in the name of Jesus Christ, for the forgivness of your sins; / and you will receive the gift of the Holy Spirit."

Now, that time has come. St. Luke tells us, "About three thousand persons were added that day."

In the Second Reading, St. Peter continues to encourage members of the Christian community to conduct themselves with patient endurance, even in the face of suffering. He asked them to follow the example of Christ, who suffered and died for us.

This idea of living within but separated from pagan society must have been an issue that was recognized as critical to the life and existence of the early Christian communities. St. Paul, in his Letter to the Romans, also touched upon the subject:

"St. Paul defines the relationships and duties that a Christian is to have toward the authorities (cf. Rom 13:1-7). He insists on the civic duty to pay taxes: 'Pay all of them their dues, taxes to whom taxes are due, revenue to whom revenue is due, fear to whom fear is due, respect to who respect is due' (Rom 13:7). The Apostle certainly does not intend to legitimize every authority so much as to help Christians to 'take thought for what is noble in the sight of all' (Rom 12:17), including their relations with the authorities, insofar as the authorities are at the service of God for the good of the person (cf. Rom 13:4; 1 Tm 2:1-2; Tit 3:1) and 'to execute [God's] wrath on the wrongdoer' (Rom 13:4).

"St. Peter exhorts Christians to 'be subject for the Lord's sake to every human institution' (1 Pt 2:13). The king and his governors have the duty 'to punish those who do wrong and to praise those who do right' (1 Pt 2:14). This authority of theirs must be 'honored' (1 Pt 2:17), that is, recognized, because God demands correct behavior that will 'put to silence the ignorance of foolish men' (1 Pt 2:15). Freedom must not be used as a pretext for evil but to serve God (cf. 1 Pt 2:16). We are dealing here with free and responsible obedience to an authority that causes justice to be respected, ensuring the common good" (no. 380).

As he writes of the suffering that Jesus endured for our salvation, St. Peter recalls the passages from the Book of the Prophet Isaiah that spoke of the "suffering Servant," "he was pierced for our offenses... by his stripes we were healed. / We had all gone astray like sheep, / each following his own way" (53:5, 7). Peter writes that "you have now returned to the shepherd and guardian of your souls."

Jesus used the image of the Good Shepherd as an assurance to his followers of his presence in their lives. The shepherd who is doing his job watches over and protects his sheep and lambs. As the Good Shepherd, who has laid down his life for his sheep, Jesus calls us by name; we hear his voice and follow him through the gate that he has opened for us as a means to eternal life.

During this Easter season we celebrate the return of the Shepherd. However, the emphasis here does not appear to be Jesus establishing himself as the Shepherd. Rather, he focused upon the willingness of the Good Shepherd "to lay down his life for his sheep" and that anyone who comes to him will not only be watched over but will be given life to the full.

Fifth Sunday of Easter

YEAR "A"

Acts 6:1-7 • 1 Peter 2:4-9 • John 14:1-12

If nothing else, the First Reading, from the Acts of the Apostles, tells the story of the continued "enormous" growth of the Church. St. Luke points out that the Church is not only growing by the addition of people from the local community. He notes that some spoke Hebrew "Aramaic" and others spoke Greek, which must have been a cause for some sort of friction within the group, even as St. Luke tells us of the communal nature that existed within the community in Jerusalem.

However, it is also the story of the appointment of the first deacons of the Church—showing the Apostles' understanding of the need for the Word of God and the Gospel message of Jesus to continue to be spread.

It is interesting to note the qualifications for these men. In Acts 1:21-22, we read the account of the eleven choosing someone to take the place of Judas. St. Peter, who is already recognized as the leader of the Apostles, tells the others whom they should set apart, "therefore, it is necessary that one of the men / who accompanied us the whole time / the Lord Jesus came and went among us, / beginning from the baptism of John / until the day on which he was taken up from us, / become with us a witness to his resurrection."

Now, there is no such restriction. The Apostles look for seven men from within the community who are "filled with the Spirit and wisdom." These are the ones who will be chosen to aid the Apostles in their work.

"Nothing that concerns the community of men and women—situations and problems regarding justice, freedom, development, relations between peoples, peace—is foreign to evangelization, and evangelization would be incomplete if it did not take into account the mutual demands continually made by the Gospel and by the concrete, personal and social life of man.[46] Profound links exist between evangelization and human promotion: 'These include links of an anthropological order, because the man who is to be evangelized is not an abstract being but is subject to social and economic questions. They also include links in the theological order, since one cannot disassociate the plan of creation from the plan of Redemption. The latter plan touches the very concrete situations of injustice to be combated and of justice to be restored. They include links of the eminently evangelical order, which is that of charity: how in fact can one proclaim the new commandment without promoting in justice and in peace the true, authentic advancement of man?'"[47] (no. 66).

Of the seven newly appointed deacons, all but two, Stephen and Philip, will fade into history. We will hear nothing more about the other five. (In fact, the only other references to "deacons" are found in the text of the Letter of St. Paul to Timothy.)

At the end of the Last Supper, Jesus told his disciples, "My children, I will be with you only a little while longer." After this, he gave them his Commandment of love, assured them that he is going to the Father and that their faith must be strong.

In response, first Thomas asked to be shown the way, and Philip asked to be shown the Father. Jesus used the occasion to remind them that he "is the way, the truth and the life," and that "whoever has seen me has seen the father...Do you not believe that I am in the Father and the Father is in me? / The words that I speak to you I do not speak on my own. / The Father who dwells in me is doing his works. / Believe me that I am in the Father and the Father is in me, / or else believe because of the works themselves. / Amen, amen, I say to you, / whoever believes in me will do the works that I do, and will do greater ones than these, / because I am going to the Father."

Jesus revealed that his words and works are those of the Father. Now, he passes them on to his Apostles. From now on, they will speak the Father's words and do the Father's work.

---

46   Cf. Paul VI, Encyclical Letter *Evangelii Nuntiandi*, no. 29: *AAS* 68 (1976), 25.
47   Paul VI, Encyclical Letter *Evangelii Nuntiandi*, no. 31: *AAS* 68 (1976), 26.

St. Peter explained all of this to the community of believers and warns that for some, all of this is a stumbling block. For those who truly believe, however, it must be the cornerstone. He goes on to write that we have been chosen...people whom the Lord claims as his own.

Sixth Sunday of Easter

YEAR "A"

Acts 8:5-8, 14-17 • 1 Peter 3:15-18 • John 14:15-21

The readings today ask us to focus on the works of the Holy Spirit. In the Acts of the Apostles, we see the faith being spread from Jerusalem for the first time. That first "missionary journey" shows the community's understanding of their obligation to preach the Gospel message. Philip, one of the seven who were chosen to help the Apostles in their work, traveled to Samaria, "proclaimed the Christ," and found great success.

The key issue here is the question of the Holy Spirit. These Samaritan people who believed in what they heard and saw were baptized. We know from St. John's Gospel and the story of the "woman at the well" (Jn 4:5-42) that the Samaritans were open to the faith. They may have been overjoyed to have the opportunity to have the message preached to them, as Jesus had done.

The Apostles (who up until now have remained in Jerusalem) heard of the success of Philip's preaching and sent Peter and John to confer the Holy Spirit upon those who were newly baptized. The situation is described in this way to show, according to St. Luke, that God the Father has placed his "stamp of approval" on the preaching and the conversions that follow.

In the First Letter of Peter we hear of the importance of living exemplary lives. The Apostle reminds his readers of the great gift they have received but at the same time realizes that they may have to suffer for their faith. He went on to write that in spite of any persecution that may be directed toward the members of the community because of their piety and hope, they should keep in mind that Jesus was put to death and now offers the faithful "life in the realm of the spirit."

"The word of the Gospel, in fact, is not only to be heard but is also to be observed and put into practice (cf. Mt 7:24; Lk 6:46-47; Jn 14:21, 23-24; Jas 1:22): consistency in behavior shows what one truly believes and is not limited only to things strictly church-related or spiritual but involves men and women in the entirety of their life experience and in the context of all their responsibilities. However worldly these responsibilities may be, their subject remains man, that is, the human being whom God calls, by means of the Church, to participate in his gift of salvation.

"Men and women must respond to the gift of salvation not with a partial, abstract or merely verbal acceptance, but with the whole of their lives—in every relationship that defines life—so as not to neglect anything, leaving it in a profane and worldly realm where it is irrelevant or foreign to salvation. For this reason the Church's social doctrine is not a privilege for her, nor a digression, a convenience or interference: it is her right to proclaim the Gospel in the context of society, to make the liberating word of the Gospel resound in the complex world of production, labor, business, finance, trade, politics, law, culture, social communications, where men and women live" (no. 70).

As the Ascension and Pentecost approach, we are called to turn our attention to the coming of the Holy Spirit and the work that we are called to accomplish by the gifts that the Spirit brings. It is very appropriate to hear from the *Farewell Discourse* that Jesus gave to his disciples at the end of the Last Supper. Jesus has already given them his Commandment to love one another. Now he is equating that Commandment with their love for him, "If you love me, you will keep my commandments" Essentially he is saying, "Love me, love one another—love one another and you show your love for me."

Just as we were told at the end of the Gospel of St. Matthew, Jesus will be with us "always, until the end of the age" (28:20), here in St. John's Gospel we hear the assurance the Jesus will not leave us orphans and that he will come back to us. This Discourse is part of the final instructions that Jesus gave to his Apostles. He promised to ask his Father to send another Paraclete, "to be with you always."

The Ascension of the Lord

YEAR "A"

Acts 1:1-11 • *Ephesians 1:17-23* • *Matthew 28:1-20*

For the past several weeks, one of the underlying themes that we have had regarding the readings and prayers is the idea of hope. We have heard it in the Acts of the Apostles, in the First Letter of St. Peter, and in the Gospels. There has been this encouragement to look forward—to anticipate a great gift. That idea of hope continues as we celebrate the Ascension of Jesus into heaven.

In the First Reading we are invited to hear St. Luke's introduction to the Acts of the Apostles. As he opens the book, St. Luke explains its purpose and in a few short lines gives a summary of the last chapter of his Gospel. He wants to convince his readers that Jesus is certainly alive; that he spent forty days speaking with and instructing his disciples.

Now, after promising that he would send the Holy Spirit, he has been taken up into heaven. This is the beginning of a new era. This is the time of the Apostolic Church, and the Christian community begins to grow.

"The Church, sharing in mankind's joys and hopes, in its anxieties and sadness, stands with every man and woman of every place and time, to bring them the good news of the Kingdom of God, which in Jesus Christ has come and continues to be present among them.[48] In the midst of mankind and in the world she is the sacrament of God's love and, therefore, of the most splendid hope, which inspires and sustains every authentic undertaking for and

---

48   Cf. Second Vatican Ecumenical Council, Pastoral Constitution *Gaudium et Spes*, no. 1: *AAS* 58 (1966), 1025-1026.

commitment to human liberation and advancement. The Church is present among mankind as God's tent of meeting, 'God's dwelling place among men' (cf. Rev 21:3), so that man is not alone, lost or frightened in his task of making the world more human; thus men and women find support in the redeeming love of Christ. As minister of salvation, the Church is not in the abstract nor in a merely spiritual dimension, but in the context of the history and of the world in which man lives.[49] Here mankind is met by God's love and by the vocation to cooperate in the divine plan" (no. 60).

After the Ascension, the disciples return to Jerusalem and the Upper Room—with the assurance that Jesus will come again. They also carry with them the directives that Jesus has given: to be his witnesses, "in Jerusalem, / throughout Judea and Samaria, / and to the ends of the earth."

We heard a more detailed account of the instructions that Jesus gave to his disciples in the Gospel of St. Matthew. With the promise of his presence, "until the end of the world," Jesus tells the eleven Apostles to go out possessing his authority to make disciples, to baptize, to teach, to do everything that he has commanded them to do.

In both accounts, Jesus leaves the Apostles with the assurance of his presence and the promise of the Spirit. It is more than encouragement; it is a commissioning.

St. Paul shared his understanding of the enduring presence of Jesus in his Letter to the Ephesians. He writes in thanksgiving that God, who raised Jesus from the dead, has given the community his Holy Spirit and prays that the hearts of all believers will be enlightened so that they may know the hope that comes from the gift.

Finally we are given a look at the coronation of Jesus at the right hand of God. There he takes his place as Head of the Church, which is his Body.

Once again we return to the Gospel of St. Matthew and the story of the Last Judgment: "When the Son of man comes in his glory, / and all the angels with him, / he will sit upon his glorious throne" (Mt 25:31).

Jesus promised that he would not leave us orphaned and that he would be with us always, until the end of the world. Let us pray, as we celebrate his Ascension, and as he takes his place on his glorious throne, that he will find the Church and all of us worthy to welcome into his Kingdom at the end of time.

---

49   Cf. Second Vatican Ecumenical Council, Pastoral Constitution *Gaudium et Spes*, no. 40: *AAS* 58 (1966), 1057-1059; John Paul II, Encyclical Letter *Centesimus Annus*, nos. 53-54: *AAS* 83 (1991), 859-860; John Paul II, Encyclical Letter *Sollicitudo Rei Socialis*, no. 1: *AAS* 80 (1988), 513-514.

Pentecost Sunday

Acts 2:1-11 • 1 Corinthians 12:3b-7, 12-13 • John 20:19-23

The fact that St. Luke gave us two very different accounts of the Ascension of Jesus should not go unnoticed. At the end of his Gospel, it appears that Luke would have us believe that the Ascension took place on Easter Sunday evening, after Jesus appeared to the eleven Apostles and the two disciples who had just returned from their encounter with him at Emmaus. In that account, Jesus tells those gathered that "I am sending the promise of my Father upon you; / but stay in the city / until you are clothed with power from on high" (24:49).

In the Acts of the Apostles, St. Luke tells us that Jesus continued to teach his Apostles over the course of forty days after his Resurrection. After he ascended into heaven, the Apostles and disciples remained in Jerusalem as they were told and waited for the coming of the Holy Spirit. St. Luke uses the first Chapter of Acts to describe for us the activities of the Apostles in those days leading up to Pentecost, the Jewish feast celebrating the end of the harvest. He also used it to show the importance of the Spirit to those who were already "eye witnesses" to the words and works of Jesus.

For the Jewish people, Pentecost was a commemoration of the giving of the Commandments on Mt. Sinai. They saw that event as the time when God established them as his people. With the coming of the Spirit, the community of believers is established as the Church.

In his account of the coming of the Holy Spirit, St. Luke tells us, in great detail, the story of the Spirit filling those who had gathered. We already know that it was common for the members of the community to gather daily in prayer and fellowship. Now, the promise of Jesus is fulfilled. He has sent the Spirit to empower the believers.

The tongues of fire and the sound of the wind are recognized as signs of the Spirit. It is interesting to note, however, that they are simply mentioned. St. Luke concentrates on the gift of the Apostles being able to express themselves in foreign tongues and that all who had gathered in Jerusalem were able to understand what they were hearing.

In the story of the Tower of Babel (Gn 11:1-9), we heard how God confused the language of the people and scattered them throughout the world. In the story of the coming of the Holy Spirit that confusion is taken away, and a unity of people is established. As St. Paul wrote in his Letter to the Galatians: "For all of you who were baptized into Christ / have clothed yourselves with Christ. / There is neither Jew nor Greek, / there is neither slave nor free person, / there is not male and female; / for you are all one in Christ Jesus" (3:23-28).

"Thanks to the Spirit, the Church is aware of the divine plan of unity that involves the entire human race (cf. Acts 17:26), a plan destined to reunite in the mystery of salvation wrought under the saving Lordship of Christ (cf. Eph 1:8-10) all of created reality, which is fragmented and scattered. From the day of Pentecost, when the Resurrection is announced to diverse peoples, each of whom understand it in their own language (cf. Acts 2:6), the Church fulfills her mission of restoring and bearing witness to the unity lost at Babel. Due to this ecclesial ministry, the human family is called to rediscover its unity and to recognize the richness of its differences, in order to attain 'full unity in Christ'"[50] (no. 431).

St. Luke's account of the events of the day of Pentecost tells us of the response to the coming of the Spirit by the disciples. St. Paul, in his First Letter to the Corinthians, tells us how the Spirit will impact upon our lives; that the Spirit will enable us to call upon the Lord.

St. John provides us with the theological explanation of the work of the Spirit. According to the Gospel of St. John, Jesus gave his Spirit to the disciples on Easter Sunday evening and, in doing so, commissioned them to continue in his work, specifically to forgive sins and reconcile mankind to the Father. Along with the gift of the Spirit, Jesus once again offered the gift of peace; they have no more reason to fear.

---

50   Cf. Second Vatican Ecumenical Council, Dogmatic Constitution *Lumen Gentium*, no. 1: *AAS* 57 (1965), 5.

"Jesus 'is our peace' (Eph 2:14). He has broken down the dividing wall of hostility among people, reconciling them with God (cf. Eph 2:14-16): this is the very effective simplicity with which St. Paul indicates the radical motivation spurring Christians to undertake a life and a mission of peace.

"On the eve of his death, Jesus speaks of his loving relation with the Father and of the unifying power that this love bestows upon his disciples. It is a farewell discourse which reveals the profound meaning of his life and can be considered a summary of all his teaching. The gift of peace is the seal on his spiritual testament: 'Peace I leave with you; my peace I give to you; not as the world gives do I give to you' (Jn 14:27). The words of the Risen Lord will not be any different; every time that he meets his disciples they receive from him the greeting and gift of peace: 'Peace be with you' (Lk 24:36; Jn 20:19, 21, 26)" (no. 491).

The Most Holy Trinity

YEAR "A"

Exodus 34:4-6, 8-9 • *2 Corinthians 13:11-13* • *John 3:16-18*

The three readings today teach us about our God. The readings paint a sort of portrait for us—a group picture of the Holy Trinity.

As Christians we believe in the Holy Trinity and the oneness of God who is Father, Son, and Spirit. Today's celebration is a reminder of our relationship with the Three Persons that make up our one God.

"In fact, when the Church 'fulfills her mission of proclaiming the Gospel, she bears witness to man, in the name of Christ, to his dignity and his vocation to the communion of persons. She teaches him the demands of justice and peace in conformity with divine wisdom.'[51] This doctrine has its own profound unity, which flows from Faith in a whole and complete salvation, from Hope in a fullness of justice, and from Love which makes all mankind truly brothers and sisters in Christ: it is the expression of God's love for the world, which he so loved 'that he gave his only Son' (Jn 3:16). The new law of love embraces the entire human family and knows no limits, since the proclamation of the salvation wrought by Christ extends 'to the end of the earth' (Acts 1:8)" (no. 3).

We know our God because he has revealed himself to us. For the Israelites he was "a God merciful and gracious, / slow to anger, abounding in kindness and fidelity." God proved who he was by offering his forgiveness every time

---

51   *Catechism of the Catholic Church*, no. 2419.

the people sinned and repented. He proved his love as he guided and protected his chosen people as they built themselves into a great nation under
his providence.

The underlying sentiment found in this passage from the Book of Exodus
tells us much more than words. There is a real relationship present. Moses
feels comfortable in the presence of the God who has shown him so much
power and majesty. First he bows down in worship but then, he is comfortable enough to ask—to invite God to remain in the company of the people as
they make their way to the Promised Land. Moses understands the paternal
love and care that God has for his Chosen People.

Jesus spoke of his relationship with the Father and promised to send the
Holy Spirit. From the Gospels we learn that God is love, and to prove it the
Father sent his only Son into the world. Today's passage from the Gospel of
St. John calls to mind the willingness of Abraham to sacrifice his son Isaac.
It also, following the celebration of the Passion and Resurrection of Jesus,
calls to mind our salvation and the Son's willingness to lay down his life for
our salvation.

In saying that "whoever believes in him will not be condemned," Jesus
shows that faith in the Father's Son is a gift bestowed upon everyone. Everyone is invited to believe; everyone is invited to share in the salvation offered to
all mankind. This is the "Good News" of the Gospels and the ministry of Jesus.

"The redemption wrought by Christ and entrusted to the saving mission
of the Church is certainly of the supernatural order. This dimension is not a
delimitation of salvation but rather an integral expression of it.[52] The supernatural is not to be understood as an entity or a place that begins where the
natural ends, but as the raising of the natural to a higher plane; in this way
nothing of the created or the human order is foreign to or excluded from the
supernatural or theological order of faith and grace, rather it is found within
it, taken on and elevated by it. 'In Jesus Christ the visible world which God
created for man (cf. Gn 1:26-30)—the world that, when sin entered, "was
subjected to futility" (Rom 8:20; cf. Rom 8:19-22)—recovers again its original
link with the divine source of Wisdom and Love. Indeed, "God so loved the

---

52   Cf. Paul VI, Apostolic Exhortation *Evangelii Nuntiandi*, nos. 9, 30: *AAS* 68 (1976), 10-11; John Paul
      II, Address to the Third General Conference of Latin American Bishops, Puebla, Mexico (January 28,
      1979), III/4-7: *AAS* 71 (1979), 199-204; Congregation for the Doctrine of the Faith, Instruction *Liber-
      tatis Conscientia*, nos. 63-64, 80: *AAS* 79 (1987), 581-582, 590-591.

world that he gave his only Son" (Jn 3:16). As this link was broken in the man Adam, so in the Man Christ it was reforged (cf. Rom 5:12-21)'"[53] (no. 64).

The opening lines of today's Gospel passage tell us of God the Father's plan and promise of salvation. Besides that, St. John wrote of the "world." Earlier, in his *Prologue*, he wrote about the "the Word, / and the Word was with God…and the world came to be through him" (Jn 1:10). That plan for salvation—for all people and for all creation—continues to unfold through the presence of the Holy Spirit.

At the end of his Second Letter to the Corinthians, St. Paul draws all of this together in encouraging the members of the community to live together in peace. He promises God's presence to those who conduct themselves as they should. In that promise, he repeats Moses' request that God remain with the Israelite people. The community is given more than an assurance. St. Paul prayed for an outpouring of the gifts of the Trinity. In saying farewell, he offered the people of Corinth the guarantee of the love, grace, and fellowship that the Father, Son, and Spirit lavish upon them and all of us.

---

53   John Paul II, Encyclical Letter *Redemptor Hominis*, no. 8: *AAS* 71 (1979), 270.

The Most Holy Body and Blood of Christ (Corpus Christi)

YEAR "A"

Deuteronomy 8:2-3, 14-16 • 1 Corinthians 10:16-17 • John 6:51-58

The God who set you free watches over you and provides food and water in the desert. Not only does he feed us, he gives us miraculous food, unlike anything our fathers have known. This, O Israel, is your God!

These words that Moses spoke to the Israelite people come in the midst of a long instruction in which Moses reminds them of all that the Lord has done. Moses spoke those words so that the people will call to mind the reasons why they should keep the Commandments that God had given and the covenant that he made with them.

God not only led them through the desert with great signs and wonders. He also sustained them and promised to be present in their lives as they prepare to enter the Promised Land.

In his First Letter to the Corinthians, St. Paul called to mind that same passage from Deuteronomy. He referred to the "spiritual food" and "spiritual drink" (10:4) that sustained their fathers in the desert. In the process of reminding the Corinthians of the history of their ancestors, Paul outlined the ways in which the Israelites fell away from their relationship with God and warns his readers that it cannot be like this with them.

He told them that we share in something special in our sharing in the one bread and the one cup. In that sharing, we are made one through the Body and Blood of Christ. At the same time, Paul cautions them to put aside their old pagan way of life. Because of their new relationship with Christ, they must turn away from participation in the worship of idols.

There may have been a question with some members of the community regarding a misconception surrounding the celebration of the Lord's Supper. This is not just another offering. St. Paul tells them that the celebration of the breaking of the bread and offering food to idols can never be seen as similar or interchangeable forms of worship!

Although this idea of "eating his flesh and drinking his blood" was new and at first difficult to understand, Jesus spoke openly and directly about the miracle that he would share with those who believe. He used plain language to explain the relationship that must exist between him and his followers.

Once again, we have a reference to the "miraculous food"—the "spiritual food" that sustained the Israelites. Now he is telling his listeners that he is that bread and that he will give himself so that they might live.

In celebrating this Solemnity of the Body and Blood of Christ, the three readings guide us to an understanding of the important relationship that we have with Jesus through the Eucharist. The *Catechism of the Catholic Church* answers the question, "What is this Sacrament called?" by saying: "Holy Communion, because by this sacrament we unite ourselves to Christ, who makes us sharers in his Body and Blood to form a single body" (nos. 1328-1331).

Our belief in the Body and Blood of Jesus is a fact. We believe. Today's celebration is a reminder of the effect brought on by that belief in the presence of Jesus in the Eucharist. Again, the readings for today's liturgy help us to understand that the Eucharist gives us life, sustains that life, and unites us as the Body of Christ.

Eighth Sunday in Ordinary Time

YEAR "A"

Isaiah 49:14-15 • 1 Corinthians 4:1-5 • Matthew 6:24-34

Until now, these homilies have centered upon the three readings from Sacred Scripture. Today, even though we find ourselves in Ordinary Time, we cannot help but turn our attention to the celebration of the Resurrection of Jesus (as we do each time we celebrate the Eucharist). More precisely, as we meditate on the events that won our salvation, we cannot help but realize how they effect us.[54]

No more than a mother would forget her child, would the Lord ever forget you. These words of comfort, from the Book of the Prophet Isaiah, are a reminder of God's presence in our lives. In their exile, the Israelite people show concern for their relationship with God. Far from home, they dwell in a land that is not their own. They witnessed or heard stories of the destruction of the temple in Jerusalem. They live their lives not knowing their future, especially in regards to the covenant that God made and renewed with them and their forefathers. They have nothing. Now the Prophet comes to them and speaks the words of God's comfort and promise.

Those words of comfort and reassurance are repeated throughout the Scriptures, especially the Gospels. During his Sermon on the Mount, Jesus instructed the crowds on how they should conduct themselves as true sons

---

54 [An excerpt from and reference to the "Alternative Opening Prayer," which appeared in the 2011 LEV edition, has been omitted here. The *Roman Missal, Third Edition* does not include corresponding text.]

and daughters of God. If they truly believe, if they recognize God as their Heavenly Father and call upon him in prayer, he gives the assurance that they will be heard.

Jesus also promised God's loving protection and care for those who place their trust in him. Our Father will give us what we need.

"In his preaching, Jesus teaches to man not to be enslaved by work. Before all else, he must be concerned about his soul; gaining the whole world is not the purpose of his life (cf. Mk 8:36). The treasures of the earth, in fact, are consumed, while those in heaven are imperishable. It is on these latter treasures that men and women must set their hearts (cf. Mt 6:19-21). Work, then, should not be a source of anxiety (cf. Mt 6:25, 31, 34). When people are worried and upset about many things, they run the risk of neglecting the Kingdom of God and his righteousness (cf. Mt 6:33), which they truly need. Everything else, work included, will find its proper place, meaning and value only if it is oriented to this one thing that is necessary and that will never be taken away (cf. Lk 10:40-42)" (no. 260).

The readings today speak of assurance and trust, but St. Paul puts a different sort of twist on this message. In writing to the community in Corinth, he speaks of his lack of concern for his situation in life. He trusts in Christ and has put his faith in the message of the Gospel. Nothing else matters. In sharing a look at his attitude toward his relationship with the world and with Christ, he makes the preaching of Jesus personal and invites the community of believers to do the same.

"Jesus takes up the entire Old Testament tradition even with regard to economic goods, wealth and poverty, and he gives them great clarity and fullness (cf. Mt 6:24; 13:22; Lk 6:20-24; 12:15-21; Rom 14:6-8; 1 Tm 4:4). Through the gift of his Spirit and the conversion of hearts, he comes to establish the 'Kingdom of God,' so that a new manner of social life is made possible, in justice, brotherhood, solidarity and sharing. The Kingdom inaugurated by Christ perfects the original goodness of the created order and of human activity, which were compromised by sin. Freed from evil and being placed once more in communion with God, man is able to continue the work of Jesus, with the help of his Spirit. In this, man is called to render justice to the poor, releasing the oppressed, consoling the afflicted, actively seeking a new social order in which adequate solutions to material poverty are offered and in which the forces thwarting the attempts of the weakest to free themselves from conditions of misery and slavery are more effectively controlled. When this happens, the Kingdom of God is already present on this earth, although it is not of the earth. It is in this Kingdom that the promises of the Prophets find final fulfillment" (no. 325).

The Church invites us to have a similar view of the material world. Heavenly Father, help us to be more like your Son so that we can share the Good News of your love!

Ninth Sunday in Ordinary Time
YEAR "A"

Deuteronomy 11:18, 26-28 • *Romans 3:21-25, 28* • *Matthew 7:21-27*

Today we are reminded that our relationship with God should be our most treasured possession and that Jesus has called us to make an active choice regarding that relationship. It is not enough to cry out, "Lord, Lord," or simply to call ourselves Catholic Christians. We must put our words into action.

In his Sermon on the Mount, Jesus outlined how to practice the faith that we profess. He taught the people how to pray, he taught them to trust in God's providence, and he taught them how necessary it was to make their faith an integral part of who they are.

"The Church has the right to be a teacher for mankind, a teacher of the truth of faith: the truth not only of dogmas but also of the morals whose source lies in human nature itself and in the Gospel.[55] The word of the Gospel, in fact, is not only to be heard but is also to be observed and put into practice (cf. Mt 7:24; Lk 6:46-47; Jn 14:21, 23-24; Jas 1:22): consistency in behavior shows what one truly believes and is not limited only to things strictly church-related or spiritual but involves men and women in the entirety of their life experience and in the context of all their responsibilities. However worldly these responsibilities may be, their subject remains man, that is, the

---

55 Cf. Second Vatican Ecumenical Council, Declaration *Dignitatis Humanae*, no. 14: *AAS* 58 (1966), 940; John Paul II, Encyclical Letter *Veritatis Splendor*, nos. 27, 64, 110: *AAS* 85 (1993), 1154-1155, 1183-1184, 1219-1220.

human being whom God calls, by means of the Church, to participate in his gift of salvation.

"Men and women must respond to the gift of salvation not with a partial, abstract or merely verbal acceptance, but with the whole of their lives—in every relationship that defines life—so as not to neglect anything, leaving it in a profane and worldly realm where it is irrelevant or foreign to salvation. For this reason the Church's social doctrine is not a privilege for her, nor a digression, a convenience or interference: it is her right to proclaim the Gospel in the context of society, to make the liberating word of the Gospel resound in the complex world of production, labor, business, finance, trade, politics, law, culture, social communications, where men and women live" (no. 70).

Moses could not make it more clear: "I set before you here, this day, a blessing and a curse: / a blessing for obeying the commandments of the LORD, your God...a curse if you do not obey the commandments of the LORD, your God." In the previous chapter of the Book of Deuteronomy, Moses reminded the people of their history and the history of their relationship with God through the law and the Ten Commandments.

The Israelite people had experienced God's power many times in their life. They saw his pillars of cloud and fire. They saw his splendor as he saved them from the Egyptians. He fed them in the wilderness and gave them water to drink. Keep his Commandments, Moses told them, and you will continue to receive the Lord's blessings.

Of course we know that the Old Testament is filled with the stories of the times when the people did not obey, did not keep the Commandments. The Old Testament is also filled with the stories of the times that God forgave the sins of his people and renewed his covenant with them.

In his Letter to the Romans, St. Paul showed his understanding of the relationship between mankind and God. He also shared his thoughts on his own personal struggle with righteousness and justification. Our redemption is a gift that we did not deserve, he wrote. However, the fact that it was freely given to those who did not deserve it, the sacrifice of Jesus made that redemption an even greater gift.

Tenth Sunday in Ordinary Time

YEAR "A"

Hosea 6:3-6 • *Romans 4:18-25* • *Matthew 9:9-13*

The Tenth Sunday in Ordinary Time is another one of those Sundays that is not celebrated every year but is often replaced, depending on local custom, by one of the "Solemnities of the Lord during Ordinary Time." The reason for telling you this is so that you can understand that the connection, the flow of the readings from the Letter of St. Paul to the Romans and the Gospel of St. Matthew, has been broken for several weeks. In fact, in any particular year we may not have heard the readings that came to us just previous to today's readings.

Today, one of the overall themes that can be found in the readings is that of putting our faith into action.

God sent the Prophet Hosea to speak to the people of the Northern (Ephraim) as well as the Southern Kingdom (Judah). He warned them that their piety was no more than the morning dew . . . here for a moment and then gone. After that, Hosea uttered a message whose theme became very familiar to the preaching of the prophets as well as John the Baptist and Jesus: "For it is love that I desire, not sacrifice."

Is this not the reason that Jesus has come into the world? He sought out those who were in need—those who were sick—both spiritually and physically, and he cured them of their infirmities.

St. Matthew has already told us that the people were amazed at hearing the message preached by Jesus, "for he taught them as one having authority, and not as their scribes" (7:29). They see him eating and drinking with those that they consider sinners.

If we look into verse 14, the question of fasting arises. Once again, Jesus answers their inquiries, and it becomes another teaching moment. Slowly, Jesus is showing them that the old ways are truly passing away.

The crowds and authorities see him curing the sick and forgiving sins. It seems that everything he does is contrary to everything that they believe or hold as truth. However, it is his telling them to "put aside the old ways" that is the last straw. They ask "why," and the response is that this is the way their Heavenly Father wants them to act, the way they are to respond. Jesus echoes the message of the Old Testament prophets. They called for true obedience to the will of the Father . . . not just empty acts of what the people and their leaders believed was reverence.

"By means of her social doctrine, the Church takes on the task of proclaiming what the Lord has entrusted to her. She makes the message of the freedom and redemption wrought by Christ, the Gospel of the Kingdom, present in human history. In proclaiming the Gospel, the Church 'bears witness to man, in the name of Christ, to his dignity and his vocation to the communion of persons. She teaches him the demands of justice and peace in conformity with divine wisdom.'[56]

"As the Gospel reverberating by means of the Church in the today of men and women,[57] this social doctrine is a word that brings freedom. This means that it has the effectiveness of truth and grace that comes from the Spirit of God, who penetrates hearts, predisposing them to thoughts and designs of love, justice, freedom and peace. Evangelizing the social sector, then, means infusing into the human heart the power of meaning and freedom found in the Gospel, in order to promote a society befitting mankind because it befits Christ: it means building a city of man that is more human because it is in greater conformity with the Kingdom of God" (no. 63).

"With her social doctrine not only does the Church not stray from her mission but she is rigorously faithful to it. The redemption wrought by Christ

---

56   *Catechism of the Catholic Church*, no. 2419.

57   Cf. John Paul II, Homily at Pentecost for the First Centenary of *Rerum Novarum* (May 19, 1991): *AAS* 84 (1992), 282.

and entrusted to the saving mission of the Church is certainly of the super-natural order. This dimension is not a delimitation of salvation but rather an integral expression of it.[58] The supernatural is not to be understood as an entity or a place that begins where the natural ends, but as the raising of the natural to a higher plane; in this way nothing of the created or the human order is foreign to or excluded from the supernatural or theological order of faith and grace, rather it is found within it, taken on and elevated by it. 'In Jesus Christ the visible world which God created for man (cf. Gn 1:26-30)—the world that, when sin entered, "was subjected to futility" (Rom 8:20; cf. Rom 8:19-22)—recovers again its original link with the divine source of Wisdom and Love. Indeed, "God so loved the world that he gave his only Son" (Jn 3:16). As this link was broken in the man Adam, so in the Man Christ it was reforged (cf. Rom 5:12-21)"'[59] (no. 64).

St. Paul took the entire argument a step further in reminding his readers of the story of Abraham. He wanted members of the Christian community to recognize the difference between the "letter of the law" and true obedi-ence. He called to mind all of the events in Abraham's life that proved his righteousness even before God made the covenant with him. St. Paul wanted to convince his readers that carrying out God's will was more important than going through the motions or giving lip service to keeping the Law; that the old ways had truly passed away.

---

58   Cf. Paul VI, Apostolic Exhortation *Evangelii Nuntiandi*, nos. 9, 30: *AAS* 68 (1976), 10-11; John Paul II, Address to the Third General Conference of Latin American Bishops, Puebla, Mexico (January 28, 1979), III/4-7: *AAS* 71 (1979), 199-204; Congregation for the Doctrine of the Faith, Instruction *Libertatis Conscientia*, nos. 63-64, 80: *AAS* 79 (1987), 581-582, 590-591.

59   John Paul II, Encyclical Letter *Redemptor Hominis*, no. 8: *AAS* 71 (1979), 270.

Eleventh Sunday in Ordinary Time
YEAR "A"

Exodus 19:2-6 • Romans 5:6-11 • Matthew 9:36–10:8

After three months of wandering in the desert, the Israelites arrived at Sinai and pitched their tents at the base of the mountain. They had seen many things over the course of those days.

Not only had God showed them signs and wonders, he parted the sea, fed them with bread from heaven, and gave them water flowing from a rock; he showed the power of his hand, first against the Egyptians and then against the armies of Ămalĕk, giving the Israelites victory over their enemies.

Again and again God revealed himself to them. The people have heard his voice and they knew the instructions that he gives to Moses. Up until now, however, nothing has been asked of them, everything to this point in their journey has been one-sided. God has done all of these things for them and has asked nothing in return—until now.

As they camped at that foot of the mountain, God made a formal covenant with the people of Israel, "Therefore, if you hearken to my voice and keep my covenant, / you shall be my special possession, / dearer to me than all other people, / though all the earth is mine."

God has done everything for his chosen people. He has freed them from their slavery. He has fed them in their hunger and given them drink. He has protected them from their enemies. Now he wants something in return. He asked the people to listen to his voice and keep his covenant—to allow him to be their God so that they will be his people.

God did not ask the impossible. He did not ask them to sacrifice their sons and daughters, as the foreign gods of their neighbors have done. He simply asks for their love.

"The gratuitousness of this historically efficacious divine action is constantly accompanied by the commitment to the covenant, proposed by God and accepted by Israel. On Mount Sinai, God's initiative becomes concrete in the covenant with his people, to whom is given the Decalogue of the commandments revealed by the Lord (cf. Ex 19-24). The 'ten commandments' (Ex 34:28; cf. Dt 4:13; 10:4) 'express the implications of belonging to God through the establishment of the covenant. Moral existence is a response to the Lord's loving initiative. It is the acknowledgment and homage given to God and a worship of thanksgiving. It is cooperation with the plan God pursues in history'"[60] (no. 22).

What is the most amazing thing about all of this is the fact that after the people have seen and experienced all of these things, even after God has shown them his power and spoken of his desire to share his love with them for all time, the people will soon revolt against the covenant.

From the time of creation we have seen the relationship that has existed between God and mankind. Even after the sin of Adam and Eve, God did not abandon us, the highest of his creatures.

St. Paul bridges the Old and the New Testaments in his Letter to the Romans when he tells his readers that "God proves his love for us / in that while we were still sinners Christ died for us."

We must ask whether Paul is only speaking about the pagans who have never known God, or whether he includes those who have or should have known God but turned away from him and refused to share in the covenant that was made and renewed down through the ages.

Jesus offered a new covenant with the people who came to hear him speak. Whether in the synagogues, on the mountainside, or along the shore of the sea. If they have the faith to come and listen—if they put their faith in what they hear—they enter into that covenant.

---

60   *Catechism of the Catholic Church*, no. 2062.

He healed the sick and had pity on those who were like lost sheep. St. Matthew uses this moment to once again share Christ's call to discipleship. Jesus sent his disciples into the world to participate in his ministry—as laborers in the harvest and as shepherds for the sheep. In doing so, St. Matthew reminds us of the covenant that has been made through the blood of our Savior and how we are called to share in this covenant as disciples of his word and work.

Twelfth Sunday in Ordinary Time

YEAR "A"

Jeremiah 20:10-13 • *Romans 5:12-15* • *Matthew 10:26-33*

We continue hearing the message of discipleship that Jesus shared with his followers. The message is as important for us today as it was for his Apostles and those others that Jesus chose to share in his mission.

Through the centuries, theologians and even the Church Fathers at the Council of Trent have argued over the meaning of this passage. Even though he did not use the words "original sin," we might interpret St. Paul's meaning as he writes that just as "through one man sin ENTERED the world…"

However, as we place this passage from St. Paul's Letter to the Romans alongside the reading from Jeremiah and the verses from Chapter 10 of St. Matthew, it takes on a different meaning. At the same time, in a way it pulls together all of these ideas of "being called to discipleship and the hardships that will have to be endured."

St. Paul states the fact that sin came into the world and there is nothing that we ourselves can do about it. Jeremiah worried about the reception of the message that he was sent to preach, and there was nothing that he could do about the way people accepted him and the "Word of God." Jesus warned his disciples that they would be persecuted, but they should not worry about it, because he has given them everything that they needed to overcome the opposition.

The common element here is the fact that being victorious over all of this—over sin, over opposition, over persecution and doubt—not only depends upon but requires the grace of God the Father.

In contemplating our own discipleship, our own relationship with the Father, we cannot help but turn to the words of St. Augustine: "You have made us for yourself, O Lord, and our hearts are restless until they rest in you"[61] (no. 114).

"This marvelous vision of man's creation by God is inseparable from the tragic appearance of original sin. With a clear affirmation the Apostle Paul sums up the account of man's fall contained in the first pages of the Bible: 'Sin came into the world through one man and death through sin' (Rom 5:12). Man, against God's prohibition, allows himself to be seduced by the serpent and stretches out his hand to the tree of life, falling prey to death. By this gesture, man tries to break through his limits as a creature, challenging God, his sole Lord and the source of his life. It is a sin of disobedience (cf. Rom 5:19) that separates man from God.[62]

"From revelation we know that Adam, the first man, transgresses God's commandment and loses the holiness and justice in which he was made, holiness and justice which were received not only for himself but for all of humanity: 'By yielding to the tempter, Adam and Eve committed a personal sin, but this sin affected the human nature that they would then transmit in a fallen state. It is a sin which will be transmitted by propagation to all mankind, that is, by the transmission of a human nature deprived of original holiness and justice'"[63] (no. 115).

In the passage of the Gospel of St. Matthew, we continue with Chapter 10 as Jesus prepared to send his Apostles to the towns and villages in search of the "lost sheep of Israel." He empowered them to share the gifts that they have received from him: "As you go, make this proclamation: / 'The Kingdom of heaven is at hand.' / Cure the sick, raise the dead, / cleanse the lepers, drive out demons" (10:7).

As they prepared to leave, Jesus gave them a series of warnings... "I am sending you like sheep in the midst of wolves" (10:16). At the same time

---

61   St. Augustine, *Confessions*, I, 1: PL 32, 661: "Tu excitas, ut laudare te delectet; quia fecisti nos ad te, et inquietum est cor nostrum, donec requiescat in te."
62   Cf. *Catechism of the Catholic Church*, no. 1850.
63   *Catechism of the Catholic Church*, no. 404.

however, Jesus shares words of comfort: "Do not worry." "You will be hated," "But whoever endures to the end will be saved," he told them.

Jesus gave his disciples three warnings, and each appears to be at a different level: "Do not worry about how you are to speak / or what you are to say. / You will be given at that moment what you are to say." "Do not be afraid of those who kill the body but cannot kill the soul." "Do not be afraid...Everyone who acknowledges me before others / I will acknowledge before my heavenly Father."

For what more can we hope? Jesus does not simply provide "comforting words" in the face of the troubles that the world may throw at us in our mission of sharing his Good News. Jesus makes a promise. If we believe; if we carry out his work; if we share his Good News; he will acknowledge us before his Father, we will have a place in the Kingdom of God!

Thirteenth Sunday in Ordinary Time

YEAR "A"

2 Kings 4:8-11, 14-16 • Romans 6:3-4, 8-11 • Matthew 10:37-42

In the First Reading today, we have the story of Prophet Elisha and the faith of the couple living in the village of Shunem. In many ways the story reflects the relationship between Jesus, Lazarus, Martha, and Mary. When the Prophet visited the area, he would accept the hospitality of this woman and her husband—just as Jesus will be seen doing with his friends in the village of Bethany.

Once again, in the Gospel, we heard Jesus as he continued in preparing the Apostles for their preaching mission in the world. At the end of today's reading, Jesus noted, "Whoever gives only a cup of cold water / to one of these little ones to drink / because the little one is a disciple— / amen, I say to you, he will surely not lose his reward."

Suddenly, the connection between the First Reading and these verses from the Gospel of St. Matthew becomes clearer. The disciples of the Word of God will have their reward.

For the past several weeks, St. Paul, in his Letter to the Romans, has been telling the Christian community how they should be living; how they should separate themselves from the pagan community, at least in their actions toward one another—not to act like or treat other members of the community as if they were unbelievers. The community may have asked, "Why?" Today we have what could be seen as an answer to the question.

Because of our Baptism, St. Paul writes, we share in the Death and Resurrection of Jesus. He has entered into an intimate relationship with us, and because of this we have been freed from the bonds of sin. The breaking of those bonds, which once alienated mankind from the Creator, has renewed our relationship with God.

"Personal and social life, as well as human action in the world, is always threatened by sin. Jesus Christ, however, 'by suffering for us...not only gave us an example so that we might follow in his footsteps, but he also opened up a way. If we follow this path, life and death are made holy and acquire a new meaning.'[64] Christ's disciple adheres, in faith and through the sacraments, to Jesus' Paschal Mystery, so that his old self, with its evil inclinations, is crucified with Christ. As a new creation he is then enabled by grace to 'walk in newness of life' (Rom 6:4). This 'holds true not for Christians alone but also for all people of good will in whose hearts grace is active invisibly. For since Christ died for all, and since all men are in fact called to one and the same destiny, which is divine, we must hold that the Holy Spirit offers to all the possibility of being made partners, in a way known to God, in the Paschal Mystery'"[65] (no. 42).

In many ways, the warnings that Jesus shared with his Apostles as he sent them on their missionary journeys were less "chilling" than what we see in today's passage. "Whoever loves father or mother...son or daughter more than me..."

Jesus knew and understood the importance of service and sacrifice. He also understands human weakness. However, he also knew of the commitment that his Apostles and followers would have to make in sharing his work of preaching the message of the Kingdom and God's love.

In warning the Apostles as he did, Jesus also reminded them of his presence, the grace of God the Father and the important role in making the Gospel message known to all people. In other words, Jesus wanted to build a relationship, not only with his Apostles and disciples and between his followers themselves. He also wanted to ensure that a relationship—a solidarity in faith—existed among all people who would accept his Word.

---

64   Second Vatican Ecumenical Council, Pastoral Constitution *Gaudium et Spes*, no. 22: *AAS* 58 (1966), 1043.

65   Second Vatican Ecumenical Council, Pastoral Constitution *Gaudium et Spes*, no. 22: *AAS* 58 (1966), 1043.

"Solidarity is also an authentic moral virtue, not a 'feeling of vague com-passion or shallow distress at the misfortunes of so many people, both near and far. On the contrary, it is a firm and persevering determination to com-mit oneself to the common good. That is to say to the good of all and of each individual, because we are all really responsible for all.'[66] Solidarity rises to the rank of fundamental social virtue since it places itself in the sphere of justice. It is a virtue directed par excellence to the common good, and is found in 'a commitment to the good of one's neighbor with the readiness, in the Gospel sense, to "lose oneself" for the sake of the other instead of exploiting him, and to "serve him" instead of oppressing him for one's own advantage (cf. Mt 10:40-42; 20:25; Mk 10:42-45; Lk 22:25-27)'"[67] (no. 193).

---

66   John Paul II, Encyclical Letter *Sollicitudo Rei Socialis*, no. 38: *AAS* 80 (1988), 565-566.
67   John Paul II, Encyclical Letter *Sollicitudo Rei Socialis*, no. 38: *AAS* 80 (1988), 566; cf. John Paul II, Encyclical Letter *Laborem Exercens*, no. 8: *AAS* 73 (1981), 594-598; John Paul II, Encyclical Letter *Centesimus Annus*, no. 57: *AAS* 83 (1991), 862-863.

Fourteenth Sunday in Ordinary Time

YEAR "A"

Zechariah 9:9-10 • Romans 8:9, 11-13 • Matthew 11:25-30

One might think, after reading or hearing the readings for this Sunday, that it is almost as if the Church gives us a moment to pause and catch our breath. "You have nothing to fear, the Lord is with you!" This could possibly be the theme for today.

All four of the Evangelists allude to the reading from the Book of the Prophet Zechariah as they tell the story of Jesus' triumphant entrance into Jerusalem (Mt 21:5-6; Mk 11:7; Lk 19:35; Jn 12:15). Salvation has come for the people of Israel; salvation has come to all people who look forward to the day of the Lord! You have no more reason to fear!

The words of the Prophet also call to mind the image from the Prophet Isaiah—one of the signs of the coming of the Messiah. For Zechariah, the Prince will "banish the chariot... [and] the warrior's bow... and he shall proclaim peace to the nations." In Isaiah we read a similar and possibly more familiar promise: "They shall beat their swords into plowshares / and their spears into pruning hooks; / one nation shall not raise the sword against another, / nor shall they train for war again" (2:5).

It is important to remember that—just as we are reminded in the readings for Palm Sunday, Jesus entered Jerusalem as Prince of Peace—as the humble

King—not with a triumphant spectacle but as the Shepherd who enters the sheepfold in order to watch over this flock.

"In the messianic oracles, the figure of a king endowed with the Lord's Spirit, full of wisdom and capable of rendering justice to the poor, is awaited in eschatological times (cf. Is 11:2-5; Jer 23:5-6). As true shepherd of the people of Israel (cf. Ez 34:23-24; 37:24), he will bring peace to the nations (cf. Zech 9:9-10). In the Wisdom Literature, the king is presented as the one who renders just judgments and abhors iniquity (cf. Prv 16:12), who judges the poor with equity (cf. Prv 29:14) and is friend to those with a pure heart (cf. Prv 22:11). There is a gradual unfolding of the proclamation of what the Gospels and other New Testament writings see fulfilled in Jesus of Nazareth, the definitive incarnation of what the Old Testament foretold about the figure of the king" (no. 379).

In the letters of St. Paul we get the idea that there was a realization that the Holy Spirit was an integral part of his life and the life of the members of the community—possibly much more so than we have in our lives today. This does not mean that the presence of the Spirit is any less now than in the early Church. It simply implies that there is a possibility that we take the presence of the Spirit for granted—more than the people of the early Church.

The reason for this might be seen in the fact that for the majority of believers, there is no day-to-day struggle to hold on to their faith. At the same time we know that there are certainly Christians and Catholics who do feel pressure...who are oppressed and threatened because of their faith, or who are not free to live and celebrate their faith openly. This is truly unfortunate, and we should never forget to pray for those people. However, those of us who are "comfortable in our faith" must ask whether we take our faith for granted...possibly in a negative way.

In his Letter to the Romans, St. Paul is writing to a community that is struggling to "rise" above the world around them and live their faith as they know they should. It is to this community and to communities down through the ages that St. Paul recalls of the presence and power of the Spirit that gives new life (cf. 522).

Before his Ascension, Jesus promised his disciples that he would be "with them always, until the end of the age!" (Mt 28:20). In today's Gospel, also from St. Matthew, we hear this prayer of praise and thanksgiving offered by the Son to the Father. In allowing us to listen, Jesus shares his knowledge of his relationship with God the Father and reveals the Father's relationship with us.

We come to know God the Father through the Son. Jesus has chosen us so that he can teach us about the love the Father has for all of his children—all of us. As he does so, he tells us to put aside all our worries and troubles. He will share his "yoke" of love and obedience with us. We are no longer empty followers. We have been given the way, the truth, and the life.

Just as the Prophet Zechariah preached hope and fulfillment to the people of Israel, the message in today's readings tells of a greater hope and fulfillment. We have been called children of God, and we know that through the sufferings, Death, and Resurrection of Jesus, this is exactly what we are.

Fifteenth Sunday in Ordinary Time

YEAR "A"

Isaiah 55:10-11 • *Romans 8:18-23* • *Matthew 13:1-23*

"So shall my word be / that goes forth from my mouth; / my word shall not return to me void, / but shall do my will, / achieving the end for which I sent it." After rereading this passage from the Book of the Prophet Isaiah, would it be fair to ask for a clarification on its meaning? What was the reason, "the end" that God was expecting after sending his Word upon the earth?

On the surface, it could possibly be argued that it simply was the proclamation of God's love…the Prophet spoke the "words" that God had given him. At the same time, it is more likely that there is a deeper meaning—one that cannot be fully understood until the arrival of the "Word made flesh."

Isaiah compares God's Word to the rain and snow that nourish the earth and bring life. In the Book of Genesis we read: "When the LORD God made the earth and the heavens—there was no field shrub on earth and no grass of the field had sprouted—for the LORD God had sent no rain upon the earth" (2:3). The rain and snow make the earth "fertile and fruitful," providing what is needed to sustain life. Just so, the Word of God is given in order to provide and sustain spiritual life.

If we have never experienced the planting, the growing, and harvesting the fruits of the earth, it may be difficult to fully understand the message of today's readings. Just as it may be difficult to understand the depth of the message from the passages surrounding the story of the Good Shepherd if we have never experienced pastures and flocks.

It is difficult if not impossible to plant a garden or a field without preparing the ground. One cannot go out and simply scatter seed on ground that has not been cultivated in some way and expect any sort of favorable results.

In the Gospel, Jesus used two images to illustrate his point. We hear one story about the seeds and another about the ground onto which the seeds are scattered. As he tells the parable Jesus draws the crowd into something familiar while at the same time giving them a reason to go home "scratching their heads" as they ponder the message.

Once we hear the explanation given to the Apostles by Jesus, the use of the images in the parable comes into focus. The Word, the message of salvation is given to us. What we do with it is another matter. If we allow the cares and troubles of the world to overshadow the message it does not take root in our lives. If, on the other hand, we allow the "Word" to find a place in our hearts and lives, it produces an abundant harvest—it fills us and continually renews itself.

"Through the gift of his Spirit and the conversion of hearts, he comes to establish the 'Kingdom of God,' so that a new manner of social life is made possible, in justice, brotherhood, solidarity and sharing. The Kingdom inaugurated by Christ perfects the original goodness of the created order and of human activity, which were compromised by sin. Freed from evil and being placed once more in communion with God, man is able to continue the work of Jesus, with the help of his Spirit. In this, man is called to render justice to the poor, releasing the oppressed, consoling the afflicted, actively seeking a new social order in which adequate solutions to material poverty are offered and in which the forces thwarting the attempts of the weakest to free themselves from conditions of misery and slavery are more effectively controlled. When this happens, the Kingdom of God is already present on this earth, although it is not of the earth. It is in this Kingdom that the promises of the Prophets find final fulfillment" (no. 325).

Although Jesus gives no more details about the "good soil," it is safe to imagine that it is ground that has been prepared, and even after the seeds were planted, the ground was tended. Here we can look back at today's reading from the Prophet Isaiah, "Just as from the heavens / the rain and snow come down / and do not return there / till they have watered the earth, / making it fertile and fruitful."

The Word—the message—has been given to us. If we accept it and make it part of our lives we have the assurance that God will continue to be present and will enable that seed to take root and grow to abundance.

Sixteenth Sunday in Ordinary Time

YEAR "A"

Wisdom 12:13, 16-19 • Romans 8:26-27 • Matthew 13:24-43

In the opening lines of Chapter 12 of the Book of Wisdom we read the author's accusations against those who in the past turned to the worship of false gods and idols. He outlines the depravity of the people of past generations as a way to show how important it is for the present and future generations to worship the one true God.

Today's passage contains what might be considered the introduction to that part of the Book where the author turned his sights on the power, mercy, and goodness of God. As the author sees it, everything good—in our lives and in the world around us—comes from God, "and you taught your people, by these deeds, / that those who are just must be kind."

St. Paul built upon the words of the Book of Wisdom by writing of the role that the Holy Spirit plays in the lives of the faithful. He tells his readers that until the coming of Jesus, there was something left lacking in creation—it was unable to reach its fullest goal.

It is the Holy Spirit, according to St. Paul, that "comes to the aid of our weakness; for we do not know how to pray as we ought, / but the Spirit himself intercedes." In a certain sense this is a radical change in what St. Paul has already shared with the community. For the past several weeks we have been hearing him warn them of the need to rise above the life that they see around them. Now it appears that he is saying that we cannot do it on our own...but luckily we have the Spirit who accomplishes these things for us.

Jesus speaks to us again about the Kingdom of God—one of the major themes in the Gospel of St. Matthew. The first of the three parables we heard today is more straightforward than the story of the sower and the seeds. It is still necessary, however, for Jesus to explain the meaning to his disciples.

Apparently the story of the mustard seed and the woman who kneads the yeast into the flour are easier to understand. Our understanding of the Kingdom begins with a small idea or thought. As we continue to contemplate its presence in our life, that idea grows until it fills us with the desire to share in it.

"The entrance of Jesus Christ into the history of the world reaches its culmination in the Paschal Mystery, where nature itself takes part in the drama of the rejection of the Son of God and in the victory of his Resurrection (cf. Mt 27:45, 51; 28:2). Crossing through death and grafting onto it the new splendor of the Resurrection, Jesus inaugurates a new world in which everything is subjected to him (cf. 1 Cor 15:20-28) and he creates anew those relationships of order and harmony that sin had destroyed. Knowledge of the imbalances existing between man and nature should be accompanied by an awareness that in Jesus the reconciliation of man and the world with God—such that every human being, aware of divine love, can find anew the peace that was lost—has been brought about. 'Therefore, if any one is in Christ, he is a new creation; the old has passed away, behold, the new has come' (2 Cor 5:17). Nature, which was created in the Word is, by the same Word made flesh, reconciled to God and given new peace (cf. Col 1:15-20)" (no. 454).

"Not only is the inner man made whole once more, but his entire nature as a corporeal being is touched by the redeeming power of Christ; the whole of creation participates in the renewal flowing from the Lord's Paschal Mystery, although it still awaits full liberation from corruption, groaning in travail (cf. Rom 8:19-23), in expectation of giving birth to 'a new heaven and a new earth' (Rev 21:1) that are the gift of the end of time, the fulfillment of salvation. In the meantime, nothing stands outside this salvation. Whatever his condition of life may be, the Christian is called to serve Christ, to live according to his Spirit, guided by love, the principle of a new life, that brings the world and man back to their original destiny: 'whether...the world or life or death or the present or the future, all are yours; and you are Christ's, and Christ is God's' (1 Cor 3:22-23)" (no. 455).

"The Church, the community of those who have been brought together by the Risen Christ and who have set out to follow him, is 'the sign and the safeguard of the transcendent dimension of the human person.'[68] She is 'in Christ a kind of sacrament—a sign and instrument, that is, of communion with God and of unity among all men.'[69] Her mission is that of proclaiming and communicating the salvation wrought in Jesus Christ, which he calls 'the Kingdom of God' (Mk 1:15), that is, communion with God and among men. The goal of salvation, the Kingdom of God embraces all people and is fully realized beyond history, in God. The Church has received 'the mission of proclaiming and establishing among all peoples the Kingdom of Christ and of God, and she is, on earth, the seed and the beginning of that Kingdom'"[70] (no. 49).

"The Church places herself concretely at the service of the Kingdom of God above all by announcing and communicating the Gospel of salvation and by establishing new Christian communities. Moreover, she 'serves the Kingdom by spreading throughout the world the "Gospel values" which are an expression of the Kingdom and which help people to accept God's plan. It is true that the inchoate reality of the Kingdom can also be found beyond the confines of the Church among peoples everywhere, to the extent that they live "Gospel values" and are open to the working of the Spirit who breathes when and where he wills (cf. Jn 3:8). But it must immediately be added that this temporal dimension of the Kingdom remains incomplete unless it is related to the Kingdom of Christ present in the Church and straining toward eschatological fullness.'[71] It follows from this, in particular, that the Church is not to be confused with the political community and is not bound to any political system.[72] In fact, the political community and the Church are autonomous and independent of each other in their own fields, and both are, even if under different titles, 'devoted to the service of the personal and social vocation of the same human beings.'[73] Indeed, it can be affirmed that the distinction between religion and politics and the principle of religious freedom constitute

---

68   Second Vatican Ecumenical Council, Pastoral Constitution *Gaudium et Spes*, no. 76: *AAS* 58 (1966), 1099.
69   Second Vatican Ecumenical Council, Dogmatic Constitution *Lumen Gentium*, no. 1: *AAS* 57 (1965), 5.
70   Second Vatican Ecumenical Council, Dogmatic Constitution *Lumen Gentium*, no. 5: *AAS* 57 (1965), 8.
71   John Paul II, Encyclical Letter *Redemptoris Missio*, no. 20: *AAS* 83 (1991), 267.
72   Cf. Second Vatican Ecumenical Council, Pastoral Constitution *Gaudium et Spes*, no. 76: *AAS* 58 (1966), 1099; *Catechism of the Catholic Church*, no. 2245.
73   Second Vatican Ecumenical Council, Pastoral Constitution *Gaudium et Spes*, no. 76: *AAS* 58 (1966), 1099.

a specific achievement of Christianity and one of its fundamental historical and cultural contributions" (no. 50).

Jesus, the man who sowed good seed, has "planted the idea of the Kingdom" in our hearts. Just as we heard last week, there are many distractions that make it difficult to concentrate on his Word. More troubling still is the fact that it is not only the cares of the world that distract us but the work of the Devil and his followers that also attempt to take us away from focusing upon our place in the final harvest of God's Kingdom.

our life and every part of our existence. At the same time, we realize that we need God's love and grace to enable us to carry out our responsibilities—both physical and spiritual.

We may not know the day or hour, but we can be prepared. We have been given the gift of faith—we have a relationship with God—a relationship to which we must cling with all of our strength. Let us pray that our knowledge and understanding of God will help us to remain prepared to meet him on the last day and celebrate forever in the banquet in heaven.

The Dedication of
the Lateran Basilica

Genesis 28:11-18 • 1 Corinthians 3:9-13, 16-17 • Luke 19:1-10

The three readings in this celebration of the Feast of the Dedication of the Basilica of St. John Lateran speak of the presence of God.

In the First Reading, we heard the story of God revealing himself to Jacob. In the Second Reading, St. Paul wrote of God's presence within the hearts of those who have been saved by Christ and who accept the Holy Spirit. The story of Zacchaeus tells us of the personal relationship that Jesus invites us to enter when he proclaimed that "salvation has come to this house."

"Every authentic religious experience, in all cultural traditions, leads to an intuition of the Mystery that, not infrequently, is able to recognize some aspect of God's face. On the one hand, God is seen as the origin of what exists, as the presence that guarantees to men and women organized in a society the basic conditions of life, placing at their disposal the goods that are necessary. On the other hand, he appears as the measure of what should be, as the presence that challenges human action—both at the personal and at the social levels—regarding the use of those very goods in relation to other people. In every religious experience, therefore, importance attaches to the dimension of gift and gratuitousness, which is seen as an underlying element of the experience that the human beings have of their existence together with others in the world, as well as to the repercussions of this dimension on the human conscience, which senses that it is called to manage responsibly and together with others the gift received. Proof of this is found in the universal recognition of the golden rule, which expresses on the level of human relations the injunction addressed by the Mystery to men and women: 'Whatever you wish that men should do to you, do so to them' (Mt 7:12)"[112] (no. 20).

It makes perfect sense to speak of our encounter with God as we celebrate the Dedication of the Basilica of St. John Lateran. At the same time, someone sitting in a pew in some distant part of the globe, might be asking, "What does that Basilica have to do with me?"

The Church recognizes the Basilica not only as the Cathedral Church of Rome but also as the oldest Catholic cathedral and thus the "first" church. The reason for the celebration of its dedication (which is believed to have taken place around 313) is that it becomes a sign of the unity among all churches and believers.

With regard to our faith, we have many things in common. These commonalities are described in today's three readings: God reveals himself to us, that faith takes root and grows upon the foundation of our love of God, we respond, and we find salvation.

Over the past several months we have been hearing, in the Second Reading, the ways by which the early Christian communities were called to manifest their faith. In the letters written by SS. Peter and Paul we heard what was expected of a people who had experienced the Risen Christ. Through preaching and the example of the Apostles, the community grew in faith. As St. Paul wrote, once the foundation was laid, someone else built upon it until the "temple" was completed.

For us, the celebration of our unity as Catholics should call to our minds the same sort of awareness that St. Peter instilled in the minds of the members of the community in Rome. He told them to be aware of their neighbors. The community was made up of people who came to believe in the Gospel, living among people who knew nothing of the love of God. St. Paul encouraged the community to continue as strong examples of faith.

We have heard the Word of God, we gather for the celebration of the Sacraments—God reveals himself to us each day. The foundation has been laid—we see its concrete example in the celebration of the dedication of a

---

112 Cf. *Catechism of the Catholic Church*, nos. 1789, 1970, 2510.

great cathedral—not just stone, mortar, and wood, but the faithful people who gather in worship, whether in Rome, or in cathedrals, churches, and chapels throughout the world. The gift of the Holy Spirit empowers our hearts to live our faith and to be strong examples of what we believe.

Thirty-Third Sunday in Ordinary Time

YEAR "A"

Proverbs 31:10-13, 19-20, 30-31 • 1 Thessalonians 5:1-6
Matthew 25:14-30

We quickly draw near to the end of another liturgical year. In two weeks we begin the Season of Advent.

We return to the days between Jesus' entry into Jerusalem and the Last Supper. Jesus has been preparing his disciples for the time when he would be taken from them. At the same time, he has been scolding the religious authorities for their lack of faith, their hardened hearts, and the fact that they have failed in their responsibilities of forming the people in their worship.

Even as all of this is taking place in the Gospel, the Church wishes to direct our thoughts to the Kingdom of God and that moment when we will be called to judgment. We hearken back to the passage from St. Paul's First Letter to the Corinthians, in which he told the members of the community that the foundation of their faith was established by the Gospel message that he preached to them—not silver, gold, or precious stones. We stand on that foundation, and we need to be reminded that none of those other things matter.

Is it not interesting then that we heard from readings that spoke of an industrious wife who is more valuable to her husband and family than any treasure? The author of the Book of Proverbs lets us know that doing good, showing kindness, being generous, and having a fear of the Lord are worthy of praise—more valuable than any treasure.

"Jesus condemns the behavior of the useless servant, who hides his talent in the ground (cf. Mt 25:14-30) and praises the faithful and prudent servant whom the Master finds hard at work at the duties entrusted to him (cf. Mt 24:46). *He describes his own mission as that of working:* 'My Father *is working* still, and I *am working*' (Jn 5:17); and his disciples as workers in the harvest of the Lord, which is the evangelization of humanity (cf. Mt 9:37-38). For these workers, the general principle according to which 'the laborer deserves his wages' (Lk 10:7) applies. They are therefore authorized to remain in the houses in which they have been welcomed, eating and drinking what is offered to them (cf. Lk 10:7)" (no. 259).

How does the Gospel reading translate for us as we examine our hearts? It is necessary to take another look at the passage from St. Luke: "The laborer deserves his payment." We have to put ourselves in the position where we go above and beyond what is expected of us…to do more than simply "playing it safe." We have to ensure ourselves a place in the Kingdom at the time of the Last Judgment.

In his First Letter to the Thessalonians, St. Paul showed us the importance of being prepared. He also reveals the hopes and fears that existed within the community during the first decades after the Resurrection.

Members of the community looked forward to the return of Jesus. They expected it to happen soon and were preoccupied with being prepared. They were also concerned with those who believed and had already died. What would be their fate? Would they still have an opportunity to be counted among the elect at the time of judgment?

Not only did St. Paul reassure them, he used the occasion to remind them that they are "people of light" and have been given a great treasure through their Baptism. This takes us back to the Gospel. The master has given "talents"—gifts—to his servants and expects something in return.

As we come to the end of the liturgical year it is good to be reminded that we too have been given many gifts. God, the giver of those gifts, expects and deserves a return on those gifts. What shall we give him? What sort of people have we become as a result of our Baptism?

Now is the time to examine our hearts and find the answers. Now is the time for everyone to be prepared for that moment of judgment.

Our Lord Jesus Christ, King of the Universe

Thirty-Fourth Sunday in Ordinary Time

YEAR "A"

Ezekiel 34:11-12, 15-17 • *1 Corinthians 15:20-26, 28* • *Matthew 25:31-46*

In our celebration of Christ the King we are provided with images of what type of King Jesus will be for us. These images—the shepherd who cares for his sheep, who seeks out the lost but is willing also to pass judgment on the flock, are a perfect way to bring the Church's liturgical year to a close.

The Church asks us to consider the end of the world. We are called to look into our souls and find those issues that might keep us from a share in the Kingdom of God. We are told of the end of the world and what will happen at the moment when we are called before the throne of our King. Fortunately for us, this King is also our Shepherd, and we will recognize him not by his golden crown but by his wounded side and the nail marks on his hands and feet. This is the King who laid down his life for his sheep (Jn 10:15).

The sacrifice of Jesus, the "shepherd laying down his life for his sheep," is discussed in St. Paul's First Letter to the Corinthians. He has already debunked the notion that Jesus was not raised from the dead. Now, in the passage that we have today, St. Paul went on to parallel the story of Adam's fall with the Passion, Death, and Resurrection of Christ. In so doing, St. Paul lets us know that the Resurrection has an impact on our lives now; we do not have to wait until the resurrection of the dead in order to realize how Jesus has already changed our lives.

The image of the shepherd appears briefly in the Gospel. It does not seem that Jesus is speaking about the shepherd in the same way Ezekiel described him. What we see here is an illustration of how certain and precise the judgment will be. Those listening to the story would have had a clear understanding of the certainty of the separation of the sheep and the goats.

It is important to understand that those who have been placed "on the left" have already been condemned—not for something that they have done—but for something that they have failed to do. They have failed to see Christ in everyone they meet.

"Human misery is a clear sign of man's natural condition of frailty and of his need for salvation.[113] Christ the Savior showed compassion in this regard, identifying himself with the 'least' among men (cf. Mt 25:40, 45). 'It is by what they have done for the poor that Jesus Christ will recognize his chosen ones. When "the poor have the good news preached to them" (Mt 11:5), it is a sign of Christ's presence'"[114] (no. 183).

It is also important to note that St. Matthew tells us that Jesus said that "all nations" will be gathered before the throne. Jesus is telling us that everyone—all of humanity down through the ages—will undergo this judgment. The story is a sobering one.

We are reminded of all of this in the celebration of Christ the King, because we celebrate the fact that all creation has been handed over to him so that it can be presented to God the Father. The end of the liturgical year is a reminder of the end of time and the Kingdom of God.

"The Church proclaims that Christ, the conqueror of death, reigns over the universe that he himself has redeemed. His kingdom includes even the present times and will end only when everything is handed over to the Father and human history is brought to completion in the final judgment (cf. 1 Cor 15:20-28). Christ reveals to human authority, always tempted by the desire to dominate, its authentic and complete meaning as service. God is the one Father, and Christ the one Teacher, of all mankind; and all people are brothers and sisters. Sovereignty belongs to God. The Lord, however, 'has not willed to

---

113   Cf. *Catechism of the Catholic Church*, no. 2448.
114   *Catechism of the Catholic Church*, no. 2443.

reserve to himself all the exercise of power. He entrusts to every creature the functions it is capable of performing, according to the capacities of its own nature. This mode of governance ought to be followed in social life. The way God acts in governing the world, which bears witness to such great regard for human freedom, should inspire the wisdom of those who govern human communities. They should behave as ministers of divine providence.'[115]

"The biblical message provides endless inspiration for Christian reflection on political power, recalling that it comes from God and is an integral part of the order that he created. This order is perceived by the human conscience and, in social life, finds its fulfillment in the truth, justice, freedom and solidarity that bring peace"[116] (no. 383).

---

115 *Catechism of the Catholic Church*, no. 1884.
116 Cf. John XXIII, Encyclical Letter *Pacem in Terris*: *AAS* 55 (1963), 266-267, 281-291, 301-302; John Paul II, Encyclical Letter *Sollicitudo Rei Socialis*, no. 39: *AAS* 80 (1988), 566-568.